The Country Kitchen

TIME-LIFE BOOKS

Alexandria, Virginia

The Country Kitchen

*country style for
the most inviting room
of the home*

A REBUS BOOK

C O N T E N T S

INTRODUCTION

6

Kitchen Style

Getting the Look

Kitchen Collectibles

The Pantry

Traditional Pantries • An Amish Pantry
Gifts from the Pantry • Space-Saving Pantries • Pantry Options
Dressing Up Your Jars and Bottles • The Butler's Pantry
Pantry in a Corner

116

Country Table Settings

Simple Is Beautiful • Mix and Match
A History of Flatware • Tabletop Surprises • Focus on Color
Setting a Country Tea • Spring Settings • Secondhand Finds
Country Shakers • Summer Settings • Country Elegance
Creating a Centerpiece • Autumn Settings
Dining Alternatives • Quilt Square Napkins
Winter Settings

134

T he country kitchen. The very words call to mind thoughts of an inviting room, simply furnished. Baskets and dried herbs hang from beams, copper pots are displayed on a wall, a fire burns in a wood stove, perhaps, and the aroma of fresh-baked bread is in the air.

With its many styles, today's country kitchen often diverges from this nostalgic image, yet its essential warmth and comfort are qualities that never change. For whether it is a large room in a rural farmhouse or a small alcove in an urban apartment, the country kitchen is truly the heart of the home.

The history of the kitchen as the center of the household can be traced to early American times. The one-room homes of the first European settlers were nothing more than kitchens in which people not only cooked and ate, but also slept and bathed. The dominant feature was the large fireplace, often as wide as ten feet, which provided all of the heat and most of the light in the room. A fire was kept burning even in the hottest weather because starting a new one with flints and tinder was a laborious process that could take hours. The few kitchen furnishings included a worktable, a bench, a chest, and a bed.

By the 1700s, dry sinks, meal chests, flour bins, freestanding cupboards, and Windsor chairs had become commonplace in kitchens, but other amenities were slower to catch on. Although the wood-burning cookstove had been introduced by the late 1700s, for example, it was expensive and its use did not become prevalent until the mid-1800s. Even as late as the 1860s, Harriet

Beecher Stowe, a popular home economist of her day, was urging a return to open-hearth cookery because she believed that using a stove for cooking ruined the taste of food.

The hardships of preparing meals in early kitchens have long since disappeared, but the sense of communion fostered there serves as the inspiration for today's country kitchen. As you will discover in this book, this versatile room may be colonial, Shaker, Victorian, or even contemporary in feeling; however, it is the homeowner's individual tastes that give the room its true character. You will also learn here how various homeowners have achieved the country look in their kitchens, often simply by selecting pretty wallpaper and traditional cabinetry or adding a few personal touches, such as a hand-painted floor cloth or a stenciled wall border.

Here, too, you will find information on some of the most popular kitchen collectibles available today—pottery, utensils, appliances, and textiles—which can be displayed as well as used. There is also a chapter on country pantries that offers ideas for storage. And, of course, no eat-in country kitchen would be complete without a table setting that complements the rest of the decor. The chapter on table settings not only gives ideas for country dishware and flatware, but also offers suggestions for making linens and centerpieces—even for serving a country tea.

No matter what the size or style of your kitchen, *The Country Kitchen* will help you make it one of the most hospitable and appealing rooms of the home.

Kitchen Style

the many possibilities for decorating a country kitchen

Today's kitchen is a popular gathering place, where family and friends are as likely to be found relaxing around the table as they are preparing a meal. And because people are spending more time in this multipurpose room, more attention is being paid to how it looks.

Country style offers a particularly wide range of decorating possibilities for the kitchen. As the following pages show, a country kitchen might be a careful re-creation of a keeping room designed to complement an 18th-century farmstead. Or, an eclectic room that displays a collection of whimsical flea-market finds. It can also be contemporary, made "country" by the use of cheerful colors and accessories: brightly painted stools or maybe a few pieces of new folk art. Antiques, of course, also have their place in a country kitchen. Where better to put an 18th-century hutch or dry sink than in the room for which it was originally intended? Whatever look you choose, you will find that country kitchen style suits today's relaxed way of life.

A hutch-table and banister-back chairs furnish a traditional keeping room kitchen.

Quaker Farmhouse

Among the simple but serviceable furnishings in the renovated farmhouse kitchen at right is an early-19th-century chopping block that once stood in a butcher's shop. The large tin canisters beside it, decorated with smoke graining, were used to store food.

This remodeled kitchen reflects a careful effort by the owners to preserve the original character of their Pennsylvania farmhouse, built by Quakers in the early 1700s.

Using local materials and subdued colors, the homeowners shaped a design based on the Quaker preference for order, practicality, and restraint. For a simple background, they whitewashed the walls, ceiling, and beams and chose plain wood cabinetry, which they painted a shade of blue similar to the original paint discovered in the farmhouse parlor.

Although iron and steel wire goods, like the footed basket above, were made in the colonies as early as the mid-1600s, they did not become common kitchenware until two hundred years later. This late-19th-century piece was used for washing salad greens and storing and boiling potatoes.

Uncovered during the renovation of their house, the original fireplace was carefully restored with Pennsylvania fieldstone and fitted with a reproduction mantelpiece. The floor was made out of the siding from a Lancaster County barn: the red-painted sides were laid face down and the unfinished tops sanded and polished.

The furnishings are also fitting for a house built around 1700. The 18th-century settle-table is surrounded by Windsor chairs, including bow-backs and one comb-back, and a rare ladder-back highchair that dates from the 1780s.

Rustic Warmth

The owners of this farmhouse kitchen replaced cabinets installed in the 1950s with rustic pieces like the sink cabinet above. The hinged countertop folds up for extra work surface.

To reflect the warm, rustic atmosphere of their 1820s Michigan farmhouse, the owners of this snug country kitchen have gathered a collection of simple, well-worn furnishings. At the center of the room, a turn-of-the-century baking table serves as a work island; stoneware pieces are stored in its base.

The unusual cabinet, above, was made from floorboards taken from the attic of the house. Purchased at a flea market, the copper sink dates from about 1830.

Well-worn furnishings, right, provide storage and work areas.

CARE OF COPPER AND BRASS COOKWARE

Admired for its rich luster and durability, copper and brass cookware has been a prized addition to kitchens for generations. Today, antique copper and brass pots, kettles, and utensils are valued for decorative display, and many collectors enjoy using them for cooking. A wide

selection of new copper cookware is also available. Brass, an alloy of copper and zinc, is a less effective heat conductor than copper and is now more often used for such pieces as trivets and molds.

Whether your copper and brass cookware is old or new, it requires special care. Because direct contact

with copper and brass can cause some foods to discolor and taste metallic, cookware made from these metals is generally lined with tin or, if the piece is new, sometimes with stainless steel. To protect the lining in day-to-day cooking, avoid using

metal spoons and utensils. When cooking over a high heat, be sure that the pan doesn't get too hot, as the extreme temperature may cause the lining to blister.

After each use, carefully wash the cookware with mild detergent and a soft cloth or sponge (abrasive soap pads or steel wool can scratch the metal) and dry thoroughly.

Copper or brass cookware tarnishes easily, but thorough cleaning and polishing will restore its sheen. First,

wash the piece in hot soapy water, then lay it on a cloth to protect it from scratching. Using a sponge or soft cloth, apply a commercial metal cleaner (or make your own from equal parts of salt, flour, and vinegar or lemon juice) and rub gently until all the tarnish is removed. It is best not to apply cleaner to crevices or grooves, however, because it is hard

to rinse out, and any residue will promote further tarnishing. Wash the piece again in hot soapy water, rinse and dry thoroughly, then polish with a soft, clean cloth.

As a rule, you should not attempt to clean heavily corroded or stained antique copper or brass at home.

Consult a professional conservator, who may be found through a museum that has a metals collection. Similarly, if a piece needs relining, contact a professional tinsmith.

You may find that new copper cookware and some antique pieces have been lacquered to prevent tarnishing. In general, lacquer is not

recommended, because it can crack or become spotted with age and is flammable when exposed to direct heat. Old lacquer is best removed by a professional using an electrolytic process, but you can remove the lacquer from new pieces yourself by immersing them in boiling water or by rubbing with acetone.

Light and Airy

The basket above is an example of a Nantucket lightship basket. Such baskets were first made around the 1850s and were so named because they were often crafted by sailors aboard the lightship anchored off the island's treacherous south shoal. Usually woven of rattan on round or oval molds, and fitted with sturdy oak handles, the baskets are prized today for their fine, close weave and durability.

This light, breezy kitchen is part of a sea captain's home built in Nantucket, Massachusetts, in the 1830s, when the island was a prosperous whaling port. Renovated by the present owners, who use the house for vacations, the kitchen incorporates as many of the original architectural features as possible, yet also captures the casual, airy feeling of a beach cottage.

To brighten the dark, north-facing kitchen, the homeowners raised the ceiling to its original nine-foot height and painted the room white.

The mantelpiece was stripped of old paint and the pine flooring repaired and refinished. Such new additions as the pewter sconces and chandelier, both handcrafted reproductions, were specifically selected to complement the 19th-century character of the house.

Creating a cheerful, nautical color scheme of blue and white, the homeowners chose simple accessories, including the china displayed on the mantel, the tab curtains, and canvas floor cloths. The delicate flower patterns on these painted "rugs" were inspired by the fireplace tiles.

An airy blue-and-white color scheme and glass-front cabinets lend an open feeling to this seaside kitchen. A drop-leaf table by the fireplace, above, makes effective use of the small space.

A Maine Restoration

Above, colorful folk-art animals and handcrafted pictures enliven the subdued decor of this country kitchen. The pictures, made by the owners, are scherenschnitte, or scissors-cut paper designs, an art form brought to America in the 1800s by the Pennsylvania Germans

Plain and tidy, this kitchen embodies a simple country spirit that is particularly appropriate to the owners' restored early-19th-century farmhouse in Maine.

Removing all signs of previous renovation—the room had been remodeled during the Victorian period—the owners created a decor suited to the 1830s, when the kitchen was added to the house. The woodwork was painted a soft gray green—a color that would have been used in that time—and simple cabinets were made from pine panels. Painted pieces such as the 19th-century blanket chest with a stippled finish, right, and the red-painted cupboard, above, are also in keeping with the period feeling.

A homespun curtain caught with a ribbon suits the farmhouse kitchen at right.

A Dried-Apple Wreath

Hung from a mantel or on a kitchen wall or door, a wreath made from dried apples can bring a warm, festive touch to your home. Any type of apple will work for this project, but Red Delicious, used here, have a particularly nice shape when sliced. The other basic supplies are also readily available—you can purchase a wreath form from a florist and an easy-to-use hot-glue gun at a hardware store.

Leave your apple wreath unadorned or trim it with ribbons, cinnamon sticks, and bows. When you are not displaying it, protect the wreath by storing it in a plastic bag; it will last for years.

A. Apples should be cut crosswise into ¼-inch-thick slices. Only slices with the star-shaped core are used.

SUPPLIES AND EQUIPMENT

· Approximately 15 large apples, preferably Red Delicious ·
· 2 cups lemon juice · 3 tablespoons salt ·
· 3 tablespoons citric acid (available at grocery stores) ·
· Cake racks for drying apples ·
· 12-inch straw wreath form ·
· Florist's wire ·
· Hot-glue gun and 1 package glue sticks ·
· 12-ounce spray-can clear, satin-finish acrylic ·
· Grosgrain or other ribbon (optional) ·
· Cinnamon sticks (optional) ·

ASSEMBLY

1. Preheat the oven on the lowest temperature setting.

2. Mix the lemon juice, salt, and citric acid in a large bowl. Cut the apples crosswise into ¼-inch-thick slices (Illustration A), saving only those slices that contain the star-shaped portion of the core. Immerse the apple slices in the lemon solution and soak for 5 minutes.

3. Drain the slices on paper towels. Lay the slices on the cake racks and place in the oven to dry for 6 to 8 hours, or until slices become leathery. Drying the slices at low heat prevents them from curling and turning brown.

4. Thread approximately 6 inches of wire through the straw wreath form, and twist to make a loop for hanging.

5. One at a time, hot-glue the apple slices (following the manufacturer's directions for the hot-glue gun) around the inner edge of the form, making sure that they overlap. In the same manner, glue more slices around the outside edge (Illustration B). The glue dries in a few minutes.

6. After gluing the apples to the inside and the outside of the form, glue more apples around the top of the form, making sure all of the straw on the front of the wreath is covered (Illustration C). Leave the back uncovered so that the wreath lies flat.

7. Spray the apple wreath with acrylic. Add a ribbon, a bow, and a few cinnamon sticks, if desired.

B. Apple slices should be glued, one at a time, on the inside and outside edges of the wreath form, overlapping slightly.

C. Apple slices should continue to be overlapped until the top of the wreath form is covered.

A Cheerful Mix

When the owners of this 1930s New Jersey home remodeled their kitchen and added on a dining area, they aimed for a homey, cheerful design rather than a specific period re-creation. To achieve the look they wanted, they combined traditional materials with a casual mix of reproductions and antiques.

Here, pine plank flooring, oak ceiling beams, and walls of whitewashed barn siding—all new additions—form the framework for the cozy decor. Because they liked its simple lines and gen-erous proportions, the owners saved the por-celain sink, original to the kitchen, and enclosed it with a new cabinet made from barn siding. Instead of built-in wall cabinets, they opted for kitchen storage units like the oak cupboard near the sink, made from the bottom half of a turn-of-the-century Hoosier cabinet.

In the dining area, above, a reproduction step-back cupboard displays antique pewter plates and coffeepots. Located by the dining table, the electric cast-iron stove serves as a convenient warming oven.

The accessories in this friendly kitchen include braided rugs, custom made for the room, and plaid swag

curtains and a tablecloth, made by one of the homeowners.

California Whimsy

A popular collectible, the fruit crate labels above, which date from the 1930s, are examples of the colorful advertisements used on wooden produce crates from the late 1800s to the 1950s.

An artful balance of humor and practicality characterize the design of this California kitchen, remodeled by an interior designer, yet marked by the owner's playful sense of style.

Chosen for its color and distinctive graining, the ash cabinetry creates a simple, light backdrop for a contemporary country decor punctuated by fanciful details. The owner, an artist, painted the wooden leaf cutouts on the cabinet drawers herself and used similarly bright colors on the cheerful stools. The eclectic look is enhanced by a wall of windows in disparate shapes. The large oval pane, found at a salvage yard, is flanked by two narrow, double-hung windows, and glass blocks form sidelights by the door.

But while it is light-spirited, this kitchen is also clearly designed for efficiency. The well-planned cooking area above includes two modern ovens, a microwave, and a refrigerator, all recessed into the wall to save space. The cabinetry, too, is practical: six-foot-tall pantry cupboards house staples and a convenient pull-down telephone desk, and open shelves hold cookbooks, toys, and trinkets. A semicircular butcher-block counter provides a place for casual dining, and the built-in wine rack next to it makes good use of leftover space.

To create an informal room, where cook and guests can mingle comfortably, the owner of this kitchen knocked out a wall and installed a countertop eating area. Whimsical details include the cherubs on the cabinets, above, and the wings and falling feather etched into the glass door, opposite.

DECORATING A KITCHEN STOOL

Whether they serve as informal seating or handy steps, stools are among the most serviceable of kitchen furnishings—but they don't have to look that way. By using a simple, decorative paint treatment, you can transform a stool into a personalized work of art. The directions on these pages are for new, unfinished wooden stools, but painting is a great way to refurbish old stools too.

The examples here illustrate the variety of looks you can achieve with such time-honored painting techniques as combing, sponging, and stenciling. Begin by applying a base coat of paint to the stool, following the directions at right, then try one of the decorative techniques explained in the captions. Any additional materials needed are listed in the captions.

For best results, use fine sable brushes, which prevent streaking.

MATERIALS

· Unfinished wooden stool ·
· Oil-base paints ·
(approximately 8 ounces for each color)
· 1 pint mineral spirits · 1 pint shellac · 1 pint flat varnish ·
· Three 1-inch paintbrushes, preferably sable ·
(one for shellac, one for oil-base paint, one for varnish)
· Fine sandpaper (optional) ·

GENERAL DIRECTIONS

1. Sand the stool to remove any rough spots, then wipe clean with a dustcloth.

2. To seal the unfinished wood, apply shellac; let dry 1 hour. Apply a second coat of shellac and let dry.

3. Apply a base coat of paint with the second brush and let dry 8 hours. Apply two more coats in the same manner.

4. To seal the base color, apply another coat of shellac and let dry.

5. Apply a painted decoration following the directions next to the individual stools on these pages. If the directions call for thinned paint, use mineral spirits to dilute the paint to the consistency of light cream.

6. Let the paint decoration dry overnight. For protection, apply a coat of varnish; let dry 24 hours and apply another coat.

Checkerboarding Using metal straight-edge and utility knife, lightly score a grid of 1-inch squares into base coat on seat. Cut 1-inch-wide masking tape into 1-inch lengths and adhere to every other square on seat to make checkerboard. Paint seat; let dry. Repeat with three more coats. Remove tape. Paint seat edge, rungs, and legs.

Combing Make comb from 1/8-inch-thick flat cardboard, 2 inches wide by 4 inches long. Cut "teeth" along one long edge at varying widths. Apply thinned coat of paint over base coat to cover seat; let stand 3 minutes. Drag comb lightly over surface with a wavy motion, exposing base color. Continue combing over entire surface of seat.

One-color sponging Rinse small cosmetic sea sponge in water to dampen; squeeze out excess. Dip sponge in thinned paint and blot on paper towel to remove excess. Dab sponge lightly over stool, allowing base color to show through.

Stenciling Make your own stencils or use stencil kit. Plan design before stenciling by positioning stencils over stool seat and back rail, and marking placement. With thinned paints, stencil one row at a time, using a small cosmetic sea sponge rinsed in water, or a stencil brush. Wipe excess paint from sponge or brush on paper towel before applying.

Two-color sponging Rinse medium-size sea sponge in water; squeeze out excess. Dip sponge in thinned dark paint and blot on paper towel. Dab sponge lightly over surface, allowing base coat to show through; let dry. Use same sponging technique to apply lighter second color.

Corking Dip champagne or wine cork into thinned paint and blot excess on paper towel. Press cork onto stool seat to leave print. Continue as above over entire seat, wiping excess paint off cork as necessary.

Artful Illusion

I n this handsome country kitchen, where rustic wood is paired with sleek French tiles, the casual look of open storage works well with the tidy efficiency of closed cupboards. While most of the kitchen gear is hidden away behind doors, decorative pieces—like the owner's 19th-century copper molds and the bread baskets atop the range hood—are kept out for easy access and display.

The kitchen's charm, however, comes from yet another type of storage: an open "pantry," above, which is *always* stocked. Created by the owner, this trompe l'oeil painting transforms a swinging door into a decorative focal point.

Both the range hood and refrigerator doors, left, were painted to match the walls.

"People have always been intrigued by illusion— anything that fools the eye," says the owner and creator of the painted "pantry," above. The art of deliberately deceiving the viewer with such realistically detailed pictures dates back to ancient Greece.

29

Above, simple lines, classic paneled cabinetry, and elegant materials, including marble and French tiles, give this country kitchen a sophisticated feeling. A muted color scheme based on white ties the room together.

Designed to accommodate a large family as well as a catering business, this spacious kitchen relies on simple, handsome materials, European antiques, and a cool white color scheme for its sophisticated country atmosphere.

Yet for all its elegant good looks, the room is also practical, efficient, and easy to maintain. Most cooking tasks are accomplished at the center island above, where utensils are easily accessible from an overhead pot rack, or at the expansive countertops along the wall. Custommade by a local craftsman, the paneled cupboards above and below the counters allow for maximum use of the space.

Selected for both the island and the countertops, white-and-gray-veined marble introduces subtle pattern into the room and offers a lasting work surface. Above the counters, the white lighting fixtures, placed unobtrusively between the roughhewn ceiling beams, focus work light where it is needed.

In the adjacent dining area, opposite, the simple lines and straightforward design of antique furnishings are particularly suited to the room's understated look. The pine settle, a Welsh piece, and the rush-seated chairs date from the 1800s. Although the standing clock has been stripped of its original finish, the owners find its "homemade" character especially appealing.

Country Elegance

*Purchased while the owners
lived abroad, the European
country antiques in the
dining area, left, include a
Danish pine table, and rush-
seated chairs once used in
an English church.
The tin chandelier is
a reproduction.*

PLANNING A KITCHEN LAYOUT

A good layout is indispensable to a good kitchen. The best kitchen designs take into consideration all of a cook's activities and provide arrangements of appliances and work areas that save time and energy.

Kitchen efficiency studies show that, on the average, cooks spend more than a third of their time at the sink and about a quarter of their time at the stove, and that walking between these two areas accounts for most of the movement in a kitchen. Trips from the refrigerator to the sink and the stove are also frequent.

From this data emerged the concept of the "work triangle." Developed through studies done at the University of Illinois and Cornell University in the 1950s, the work triangle is a basic principle you can apply to a kitchen layout. The idea is to keep work centers close enough to each other for convenience but not so close that you continually have to be washing the dishes to make enough room to cook.

The work triangle is measured from the center points of the sink, stove, and refrigerator. In an ideal triangle, the sum of the three sides should add up to at least 12 feet but not more than 22 feet: the sink should be 4 to 6 feet from the stove and 4 to 7 feet from the refrigerator; the stove should be 4 to 9 feet from the refrigerator. Traffic through the kitchen should bypass the work triangle, thus preventing collisions with the cook.

In a rectangular space, the work triangle generally dictates one of three basic kitchen arrangements—the galley, the L-shape, or the U-shape—but each of these layouts can

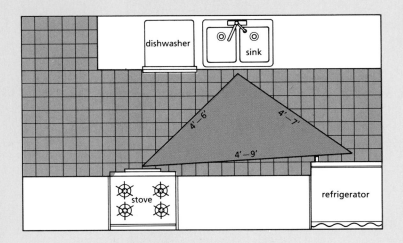

The galley kitchen Best suited to a cul-de-sac, the galley should be at least 8 feet wide to accommodate traffic and allow for opening cabinet and appliance doors. Here, as in other triangles, the dishwasher may be to the left or the right of the sink. The galley's storage is often augmented with a pantry at the dead end.

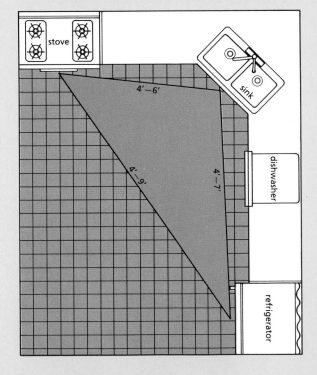

The L kitchen Here the sink, stove, or refrigerator can be placed at a right angle to the other two to form a traffic-free work triangle. Or you can put the sink in the corner between the refrigerator and stove as shown here.

have many variations. One of the sides of the triangle may be a peninsula, for example; or a side may be broken into sections by walkways or doorways; or an island may be added to the basic plan.

The galley, or corridor, kitchen is particularly efficient because the work triangle can be figured precisely with appliances on the two opposing walls. The best arrangement in this long, narrow space is to center the sink on one side of the room and place the refrigerator and stove on the opposite side, leaving counter space between the two appliances.

In the ideal L-shaped kitchen, the sink, stove, or refrigerator is placed at a right angle to the other two; or two of the appliances are situated at right angles to each other, with the third located in the corner between them. Either arrangement creates a successful work triangle near the corner, conveniently out of the way of traffic.

The U-shaped kitchen is the most popular kitchen plan. By placing the sink, stove, and refrigerator on three different walls, this configuration leaves plenty of room for countertops and cabinet storage while creating a compact work triangle.

Adding a work island to the U-shaped plan affords additional countertop area and the possibility of putting in an extra cooktop or sink. This plan works well in a large kitchen, where the corners of a single work triangle would be too far apart. Here several independent triangles may be designed, either with matching facilities to serve two or more cooks, or with special appliances or fixtures for tasks such as baking and canning.

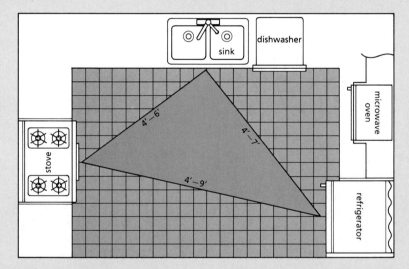

The U kitchen In this layout, the work triangle is enhanced by the flexible placement of the major appliances along the base and legs of the U. If you have a microwave oven, it is best placed near the refrigerator for convenience.

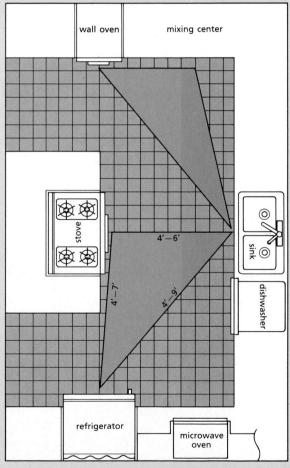

The U with island The basic U-shaped plan with an island allows for two work triangles: one standard and one for a specialized work center.

Simplicity

A dded on to a seaside cottage in 1900, this simple kitchen was recently renovated with respect for its turn-of-the-century roots. To preserve its character, the owner retained many of the original elements —including the wainscoting in the cooking area, left, and in the dining area, above—and rejuvenated the room with a coat of white paint. While cooking is done on a new range, the cast-iron stove was saved for its period look.

Framed prints, from a 19th-century book on shells, bring pattern and visual interest to the dining corner above.

Painted white, pine wainscoting preserves the turn-of-the-century feeling of this seaside kitchen.

Among the secondhand furnishings in this country kitchen are the pine drop-leaf table, right, purchased at a flea market—the bright red paint was discovered under a layer of old linoleum—and the cast-iron cookstove above.

Eclectic and quirky, this informal kitchen—located in a converted barn attached to a New York farmhouse—draws its appeal from a mix of bright colors and an intriguing jumble of kitchenwares and collectibles. "I wanted a kitchen that would be easy to live in," notes the homeowner, who purchased most of her furnishings and kitchenware at flea markets and auctions.

While she has a penchant for whimsical pieces like the wooden lawn ornaments on the wall, her kitchen "collection" is not limited to small finds. Both the sink, and the marble countertop, which is from an old pharmacy, were found at yard sales, as was the wood-burning cookstove, now converted to gas.

Casual and Cozy

Moved indoors, lawn ornaments like the romping dog above become sculptural room decorations. Made in the 1920s and 1930s, such simple, cartoonlike silhouettes of painted wood were originally designed to stand in the ground on metal spikes.

WOOD-BURNING COOKSTOVES

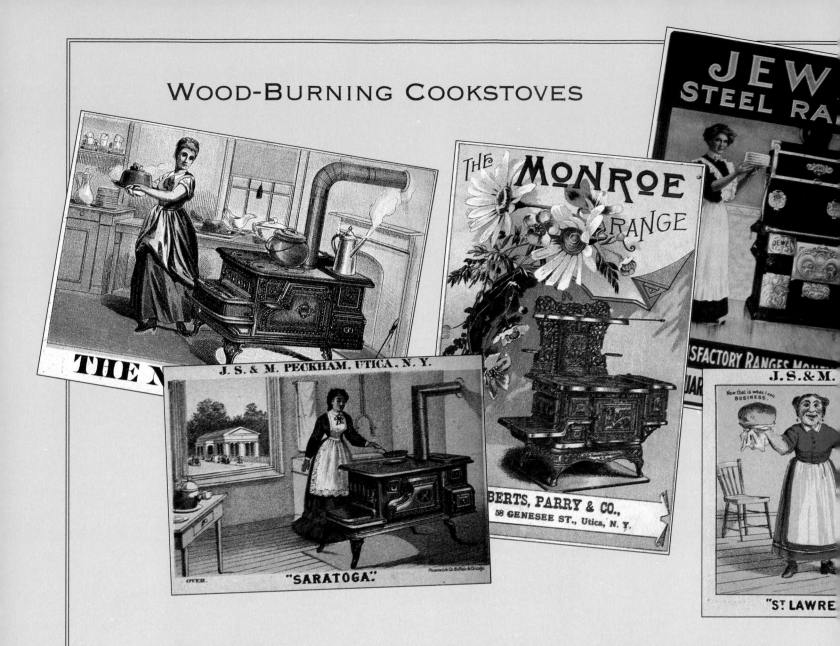

When the wood-burning cook-stove made its debut in America around 1830, it was heralded by its manufacturers as the "first major revolution in cooking since the discovery of fire." Soon cooks across the country were simmering, sautéing, roasting, and baking food—and heating their homes—using cast-iron stoves that boasted names like Country Charm, Home Parlor Cook, and Home Clarion.

Today wood-burning cookstoves still have a place in the kitchen, often sharing space with the electric range and the microwave. While some people enjoy cookstoves for their nostalgic appeal, those who actually cook on them find that the food can be especially delicious.

Vintage cookstoves can be purchased at auctions or antique shops, and handsome reproductions are widely available from manufacturers. While a new stove is guaranteed to work, an old one may have problems. Before buying an old cookstove, check for rust, warps, and cracks, and for missing pieces that may be difficult to replace.

Because a cookstove generates a great deal of heat, it requires more clearance than a regular range. It should sit approximately three feet from an unprotected combustible wall and at least eighteen inches off the floor, preferably on heat-resistant tiles. And, of course, it must be linked to a chimney.

Whether old or new, most wood-burning cookstoves generally consist of a firebox, an oven, a large cooking surface with two to eight cooking lids, a stovepipe, drafts and dampers for controlling the heat, and, on

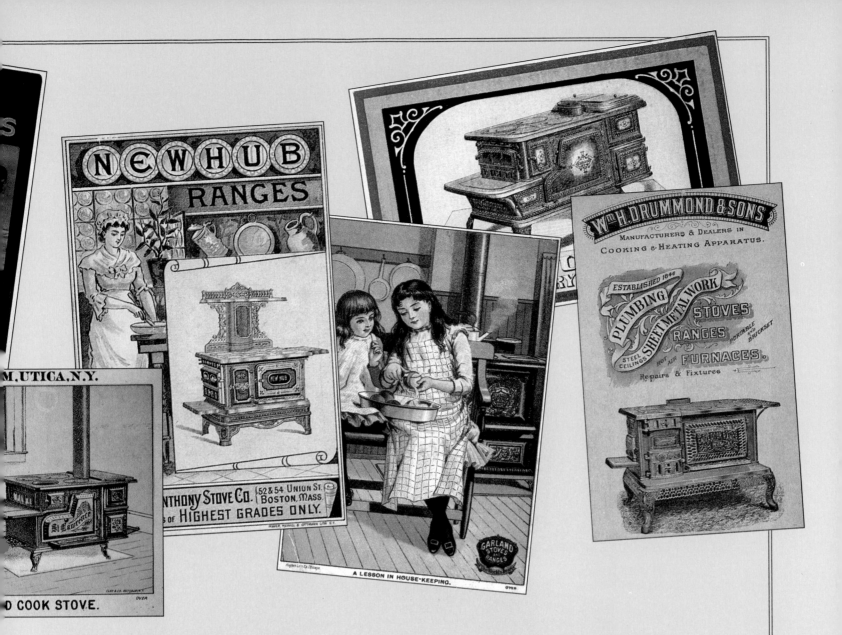

A LESSON IN HOUSE-KEEPING.

some models, a water reservoir and warming oven.

To fuel a stove you will need softwoods such as poplar or pine for kindling, and seasoned hardwoods such as ash or maple for keeping the cooking fire going. Five to six cords of wood will last a year if the stove is used every day.

Patience and a desire to experiment are the primary requirements for mastering wood-stove cookery. Every stove heats differently, but most cookstove ovens can take thirty to forty minutes to reach 350°. To

control the temperature, you will have to learn how your fuel burns and how to adjust the drafts and dampers accordingly.

Cooking on the stove surface is a lot easier to master than baking. To reduce the heat under your fried eggs, for example, you can simply move them from a hot area of the stove to a cooler one. To bake the perfect cake, however, you will have to learn to gauge the oven temperature. Some expert wood-stove bakers rely on sticking a hand quickly into the oven; most prefer to use

a conventional oven thermometer.

If you use your cookstove often it will require maintenance. Any removable parts should be cleaned weekly. The ductwork ought to be cleaned out at least once a year, since creosote and soot build-up in the stovepipe and chimney can lead to a fire. If you don't want to do the dirty work yourself, contact a chimney sweep or your local fire department.

Many of the old cookstoves featured in these early advertisements can still be purchased today.

The Shaker Way

Cleverly designed built-in storage allows no wasted space in the Shaker-style kitchen at right. Spice drawers are fitted into the island behind the cooktop, and open shelves near the desk hold cookbooks.

When the owners of this 19th-century New England cottage outgrew their small kitchen, they decided to expand it with an open-plan addition. Because the kitchen would be visible from other first-floor rooms, the owners wanted a distinctive look, yet one that was still simple, neat, and unobtrusive enough to blend with the rest of the house. The design aesthetic of the Shakers, founded on order and quality of craftsmanship, seemed the perfect choice.

The cherry cabinetry that fits precisely into the cooking center and desk area, above and opposite, recalls the carefully planned wall cupboards that the Shakers built in their homes and workshops to keep their belongings out of sight. To maintain a tidy, unified appearance in this kitchen, small appliances are hidden behind sliding panels to the right of the sink, and tiny drawers behind the cooktop hold herbs and spices. Floor-to-ceiling cupboards are fitted with drawers and shelves to hold linens and foodstuffs, and exterior shelves are built into a cupboard for books. Yet despite the many dif-

Continued

Simple white laminate countertops provide a practical work surface, yet do not detract from the beauty of the woodwork. For a unified appearance, the dishwasher and refrigerator are faced with the same cherry wood used for the cabinetry.

The angled window wall, above, brings a feeling of expansiveness to this sunny kitchen. In keeping with the plain look, the owners left the windows bare of curtains.

ferent sizes of drawers, doors, compartments, and shelves, the components are so simply proportioned and well integrated that they form a harmonious whole. Even the wooden knobs—the Shakers believed brass hardware was too "worldly" to use—tie in with the overall look.

The kitchen is also successful because of its appealing, carefully planned layout. Lined with double-hung windows, which let in plenty of daylight and maximize the view, the angled exterior wall adds to the feeling of spaciousness. In the center of the room, the step-back island offers a casual spot for friends to gather while the cook is at work. The tall stools, designed with single, gracefully curved back splats and simple cone finials, are also adapted from a typical Shaker design. Neat and trim, they make an appropriate finishing touch to a room that offers a fitting response to the adage, "A place for everything, and everything in its place."

KITCHEN LIGHTING

Although its role is often overlooked, proper lighting is, in fact, one of the most important considerations in planning any kitchen. The most effective kitchen lighting should be glare- and shadow-free, but your own particular requirements will depend on the size, layout, ceiling height, and overall color of the room. As a rule, a combination of three types of artificial lighting—general, task, and accent—works best.

The purpose of general lighting is to provide a comfortable level of overall, diffuse illumination that is bright enough to let you see into cupboards and drawers. Ceiling-mounted track lights and recessed canister lights, which can be used to supplement traditional fixtures like chandeliers and wall sconces, are good possibilities for general lighting. Both track and recessed fixtures are best installed parallel to work counters and two to three feet from a wall. You should have a minimum of 100 watts of incandescent light or 40 watts of fluorescent light for every 50 square feet of kitchen space. (Fluorescent bulbs supply about three times more light than incandescents for the same amount of electricity.) Traditionally, incandescent bulbs have been preferred for general lighting because they provide a warm light, but flattering "warm-white" full-spectrum fluorescents, which approximate natural daylight, are also available now.

Designed for specific functions, task lighting provides bright, shadowless illumination for work surfaces such as counters, stovetops, and sinks. Two-track, recessed, or pendant ceiling fixtures with 75-watt reflector bulbs are usually ample for lighting the sink. To illuminate a countertop, a fluorescent strip bulb, which can be mounted on a wall or underneath the front edge of a hanging cabinet, is an excellent choice. A lighted range ventilating hood with at least 40 watts of illumination is a good solution for lighting your stove.

Accent lighting is designed to focus attention on the special features of the room, such as collectibles, tabletops, and plants. Ceiling-mounted track fixtures or recessed lighting with spotlight bulbs work well. Low-volt halogen bulbs are also effective, as they emit a strong, tightly controlled beam.

Log Cabin Living

The owners of the rustic cabin at right decorated their kitchen with such appropriate country collectibles as blue-and-white graniteware and stoneware crocks. Now filled with spices and herbs, the glass-front panels on the old seed counter, recycled as a kitchen island, were originally used to identify the goods stored inside.

Having always wanted to live in a log house, the owners of this Mississippi home fulfilled their dream by dismantling two 19th-century log cabins, moving them to a new location, and rebuilding them as one. This cozy kitchen reflects their desire to preserve the simple character of a cabin interior while creating a livable room.

For storage, they devised rustic wall cupboards from southern heart pine boards they found in the loft of one of the cabins; the panels, made of tin roofing material, were pierced by the

44

Water coolers, or "fountains," like this one decorated with raised flowers, were usually priced according to capacity; in the 1830s, similar coolers sold for twenty-four cents per gallon. This piece bears the pebbled texture typical of salt-glazed stoneware, so named because salt is thrown into the kiln during firing and bonds with the clay to form a glossy surface.

homeowners to resemble the decorative patterns on pie safes. Additional storage is provided by two antique pieces that might well have been used in a cabin—a 19th-century painted cupboard and a set of stepped shelves that wrap neatly around a wall corner.

The center island and the stove were chosen for their utility and convenience. The former is an early 1900s seed counter once used in a country store; its deep drawers now hold cookware and linens. The cast-iron stove is actually a modern electric range.

A Live-in Kitchen

Thisremodeled kitchen is a comfortable, updated version of a "keeping room," the traditional center of the 17th- and 18th-century household. "We wanted a warm, live-in kitchen," say the owners, who use the room not only for cooking and eating, but also for entertaining guests and relaxing by the fire.

At one end is an efficient cooking area, planned around a central island fitted with a range and a laminate countertop designed to look like slate. Stained walnut cabinetry and a cherry butcher-block countertop run along the walls. To retain the low, original windows without sacrificing work space, standard-height counters were simply placed in front. The resulting windowsill "wells" now hold planters.

A new addition to the house, the adjoining sitting and dining area, above, was designed with deeply recessed windows and rough plaster walls. Here, a cozy wing chair and a pine dining table are pulled close to the fireplace, which the owners use throughout the winter. Framed by an arched opening to resemble a beehive baking oven, the fireplace was built well above the floor so that the flames can be seen from anywhere in the room. The decorative tiles are Mexican.

Located in an 18th-century Pennsylvania farmhouse, this new keeping room kitchen incorporates the

efficient work area at left and the comfortable sitting area above. The convenient height of the fireplace

makes it easy to light and keep clean.

Getting the Look

*how to bring country style
to your kitchen*

Whether you are making a few changes or have a major renovation in mind, decorating a country kitchen means considering the same essentials you would for any kitchen plan: floors, walls, cabinets, counters, storage, and lighting. Each one of these elements is important to the overall appearance of the room, and each one can give your kitchen a country feeling.

In this chapter, you will learn about the wide range of materials available today—from wood paneling to ceramic tiles—that lend themselves to country decorating. Here, too, are ideas for storage, as well as information about decorative paint treatments, such as sponging and graining, that can be used equally effectively on cabinets, walls, and floors. Start small, by painting a cupboard, perhaps; you will soon want to move on to creating a country kitchen complete in all its details.

A new kitchen gains a country look from salvaged 18th-century wall paneling.

Country Cabinets

In the kitchen at right, bright red woodwork sets off the pierced-steel panels of the kitchen cabinets, which were designed to be the focus of the room. The decorative pineapple patterns vary slightly with the size of the cabinet doors.

Of all the elements to consider when planning your kitchen, cabinets may deserve the most attention. Providing both storage and display, they are not only important to the function of the space, but also to the decor: their design can affect the appearance of the entire room. Today, a wide range of country looks is possible for cabinets, whether you purchase them ready-made or build and decorate them yourself.

When they remodeled their eighty-year-old Virginia home, the owners of the country kitchen at left based their imaginative cupboard designs on the pierced-tin panels found in early American pie safes. Decorated with a pineapple motif—chosen because it is a traditional symbol of hospitality—the galvanized steel panels were made at home by one of the owners, who punched out the patterns with a chisel and awl.

The panels were then sanded, waxed, and buffed for a polished pewter look and fitted into brightly painted stock frames. To give the woodwork a durable satin finish, the homeowners applied a coat of latex primer, followed by a coat of semigloss red enamel, then ten coats of polyurethane.

Equally traditional in style, yet very different, the simple cupboards above recall the elegant austerity of Shaker woodwork, which is characterized by unadorned surfaces and precise, harmonious proportions. The stark beauty of these painted cabinets is accentuated by their dramatic, dark green color, repeated in the adjacent window trim.

The straightforward simplicity of the Shaker-style cabinets above is emphasized by the dramatic contrast between their dark green color and the room's white walls. Green accessories were chosen to tie in with the color theme.

The stenciled design on the cupboard above deliberately echoes the colors of the wallpaper. The corner decorations are a detail from the main stencil pattern.

A good way to give your kitchen a new look without remodeling is to enhance your cabinets with a decorative paint treatment. Painting can add color and character to even the most uninteresting surfaces. While professional paint specialists will do the job for you, many techniques, such as stenciling, graining, sponging, and spatter-painting, are easy to learn yourself.

To transform plain cabinetry with bold decorative detail, for example, consider applying a pretty stencil design. You can cut your own stencils—inspired, perhaps, by a pattern on wallpaper or fabrics in your kitchen—or use precut stencils to create a pattern like that on the simple cupboard above.

For a softer look, you might try antique grain-painting, which was used to achieve the muted, pale blue finish on the kitchen cabinets at right. Here, the color of the cabinets was continued on the window trim and was also picked up in the tiles used for the backsplash.

Decorative Paint Treatments

A decorative technique called antique grain-painting was used on the cabinets at left. After a slow-drying blue glaze was painted over a blue undercoat, the grain pattern was marked into the wet finish.

Glass-Front Cabinets

Glass-front cabinets offer an ideal compromise between open kitchen shelves and closed cupboards: they allow you to exhibit decoratively packaged foodstuffs and your favorite dishware while protecting them from dust. And if you like the look of glass but prefer to keep the contents of your cupboards out of sight, you can line the doors with decorative curtains.

The new birch cabinets opposite were designed for a renovated 1900s farmhouse kitchen. The proportions of the glass panes set in the tops of the cabinets repeat those of the panes in the back door to give the cabinets a traditional feeling.

Color, too, is important to the appearance of these cabinets. The deep red paint chosen for their interiors acts as a strong contrast to the softer hues used on the walls and trim throughout the rest of the kitchen, and purposely draws attention to the shelves.

In the cupboard above, tomato red paint harmonizes with both the dishes and the flowered material that lines the doors. When the removable pleated curtains, attached with fastening tape, are taken off, the cupboard becomes a showcase for a display of handsome china.

The pleated curtains used on the doors above can easily be removed for cleaning. The fabric is attached at the top and bottom by strips of fastening tape that adhere to corresponding strips on the doors.

White trim emphasizes the simple design of the new glass-front cabinets, opposite, which enhance the traditional look of a renovated kitchen in Maine.

PRETTY SHELF TRIMS

A quick, clever way to dress up your kitchen or pantry, pretty trimmings provide a finishing touch to any shelves and offer a particularly pleasant surprise when cupboard doors are opened. The three shelf trims shown at left are inexpensive and easy to make and can be attached to the fronts of your shelves with double-stick tape.

Scherenschnitte, the traditional Pennsylvania-German craft of scissors-cutting, was the inspiration for the imaginatively trimmed top shelf. The trim here is cut from newspaper—which early American housewives often used to decorate their pantry shelves—but you can also use wrapping paper or construction paper. Simply cut a strip of paper to the width desired and to the length of the shelf (or attach separate pieces with clear tape to make up the length), and fan-fold about five times. Using short-bladed, sharply pointed scissors, cut through the layers to create a design, which will be repeated when the paper unfolds.

A wallpaper border, available at decorating and paint stores, was used to trim the second shelf. You can use a border alone or back your shelves with wallpaper and pick a border that coordinates.

On the bottom shelf, a washable window valance is put to new use as trim. Sold by the yard, such lace can be found in sewing stores or can be purchased through catalogs. Its texture and scalloped edge soften the look of the shelf.

Wood Planking

Roughhewn ceiling beams and a peninsula faced with old boards contribute to the rustic atmosphere in the country kitchen at right.

Rough and weathered woods give these two kitchens their unmistakable country feel. In the kitchen at left, boards salvaged from old stairs were used to face the work peninsula, which serves for both dishwashing and storage. The irregularly stained planks make an interesting contrast in color and texture to the ceramic tile countertop.

For a warm country look, the owner of the kitchen above chose rough-sawn cedar for the walls and cabinets. The planks were rubbed with white paint to lighten them in a process known as pickling, then coated with polyurethane to make them stain resistant and easy to wipe clean. White ceramic tiles from France and simple door pulls go well with the rustic wood.

In the kitchen above, cedar planks make an effective backdrop for a collection of brass utensils, including three 18th-century French skimmers.

Country Wallpaper

Flower-sprigged wallpaper enhances the warm, sunny atmosphere in the kitchen nook above. Displayed on a drying rack, blue spongeware china heightens the bright country look.

One of the easiest ways to achieve a country look in your kitchen is to paper the walls with a small floral print. Such delicate and cheery wallpaper, reminiscent of calico fabrics, is available in a wide variety of colors and patterns and can be used to create interesting effects.

In the kitchen at right, for example, rose-print paper was extended from the walls up onto the ceiling to make the room feel larger. In a more traditional use, the sunny floral print above was paired with a painted wood wainscot.

Green trim and laminate counters coordinate with the wallpaper in the kitchen at right.

CREATIVE PEGBOARDS

Transforming ordinary pegboard into a focal point of your kitchen is easy if you consider color, texture, and the objects to be displayed, just as you would when decorating an entire room. The result? Storage that is both accessible and eye-catching.

Sold in standard four-by-eight-foot sheets at lumber stores, pegboard can easily be cut to the size you want with a hand saw (most stores will even cut it for you). Cover a whole wall, or put small panels over a sink or stove, on the back of a door, or in the pantry. Use a mounting technique suitable to your surface or wall structure.

It is best to paint your pegboard before mounting it, however, using semigloss paint, which can be applied with a roller or brush, for an easy-care surface. Choose a paint color that highlights what you want to display. Once the paint is dry, lay the pegboard on the floor and place the objects on it, moving them

On the pegboard at top, small flat-backed baskets and a wooden spice chest provide storage for everyday household supplies and party goods. Line the baskets with fabric or paper so that small items will not fall through. At bottom, a yellow pegboard goes well with the pale colors of china, tea towels, and tinware.

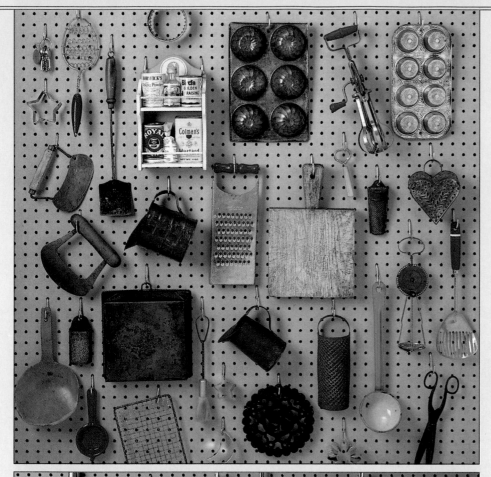

around carefully until you find an arrangement you like. Take into account the wide variety of pegboard attachments available—among them, small and large hooks, rings, and racks—but don't let that limit you.

You might also consider hanging baskets or other containers on the pegboard. Children's decorated metal sand pails, vintage bucket-shaped tins (peanut butter and candy once came in such containers), and colorful miniature shopping bags, available where gift wrap is sold, can be used to hold cutlery, linens, recipes, mail, and miscellany.

Besides being a handy storage solution, a pegboard is also the perfect showcase for your kitchen collectibles or other pieces. You can mount a single theme collection—cookie cutters, cutting boards, or trivets, perhaps—or group an assortment of odd objects, such as framed labels, bunches of dried herbs, and homespuns.

Whether grouped by use, shape, or color—or even randomly—kitchen utensils like those at top lend themselves to the puzzlelike possibilities of pegboard display. At bottom, a richly colored background sets off a collection of polished copper and anodized aluminum pans. You can outline each pot with a felt-tip pen for easy replacement after use.

Built-in Storage

The folding storage unit above serves as a built-in pantry where spices and other goods are stocked. The two center doors swing together to reveal additional shelves behind.

Essential to good kitchen design, well-planned storage can minimize work and maximize space. In this remodeled kitchen, where open and closed storage are combined, the commodious center island at right serves as the organizational focus. Here, cupboards and drawers hold cooking and household items, and the rack above keeps pots and pans within easy reach. Additional built-ins, like the folding storage pantry above, are disguised in the walls of the room. The hinged unit provides triple the space of a typical closet.

The center island at right accommodates a cooktop, work space, and ample storage.

Made to Measure

Having good storage was so important to the owners of this sleek country kitchen that they devoted twelve years to planning its design. The result is a beautifully organized space, with a special storage place devised for every pot, pan, utensil, and dish: all are on hand, yet out of sight.

Each object was first measured so that a drawer or cabinet would fit it precisely. For example, the owners use the long drawers at the bottom of the marble-topped window counter, opposite, to house rolling pins and platters. There are also specialized drawers for small items, like measuring cups, sifters, and graters, as well as swing-up platforms for heavier appliances. Wooden plates have a home in divided bins below a window seat, and metal-lined drawers hold produce and flour. Even the spice drawers are specially designed, with angled shelves for convenient access.

Above, specialized storage includes, clockwise from top left: a mixer cabinet with swing-up platform; bins for storing woodenware; a spice drawer with tilted shelves; and lined food bins, pierced for ventilation.

This contemporary country kitchen provides optimum storage in an elegant, easy-care setting.

Furniture as Storage

Practical and versatile, the furniture in early American kitchens was used for seating, serving, and food preparation—and also for storage. Today, antique benches, chests, hutches, and cupboards still have an important place in the country kitchen, providing storage as effectively as conventional modern cabinetry.

To emphasize the farmhouse look of the kitchen above, mid-19th-century furniture was chosen to hold dinnerware and to display collectibles. The bucket bench to the right of the

dining table would originally have held crocks of milk or cream and buckets of water. Here, it is used for displaying antique stoneware jugs. More stoneware appears on the step-back cupboard, where cookbooks are kept free of dust behind glass-paned doors.

The corner cupboard, embellished with a carved scroll design, makes good use of an awkward space. Next to it hangs a wooden spice chest. In early America, spices, which were imported and therefore costly, were carefully stored and often kept secure under lock and key.

In the kitchen at left, antique furniture, including a bucket bench and step-back cupboard, provides storage and display space. The owner's collection of stoneware features jugs—which once held such kitchen staples as molasses, cooking oil, and vinegar—and large storage crocks.

AMERICAN PIE SAFES

The two-drawer walnut-and-poplar pie safe above left, from Greene County, Tennessee, was made between 1830 and 1860. The old blue and red paint on the tin panels makes this piece rare. The panels on the pie safe above right show a simple, single-star motif that is set off by the pale green buttermilk paint on the pine frame. The safe was probably made in western Pennsylvania or Ohio between 1840 and 1860.

Pie safes are symbols of a time few of us recall—a time when there was little or no home refrigeration, and a time when the main meal of the day was served at noon because farm hands needed nourishment to face an afternoon in the fields.

After the midday meal was finished, the leftovers were placed in a pie safe (more properly known as a food or meat safe) to form the basis for a light evening supper. A common fixture in American households in the 19th and early 20th centuries, safes were suitable for a few hours of storage because their ventilated side and door panels kept insects off the food yet allowed air to circulate.

American pie safes may trace their origins to the English larder cupboard, which was made with panels of zinc, woven rattan, wood, or wire. Placed in the pantry, the larder cupboard was in use by the 1700s in both Europe and America.

Safes ventilated with perforated tin—rather than zinc or rattan—began to appear in America in the 1800s. Most were made by hand until after the Civil War. Small furniture shops turned out pieces in pine, poplar, walnut, and cherry, while the backyard craftsman tended to use any wood that came to hand. After 1865, mass-produced pieces also found their way into kitchens. These were more commonly built from a combination of woods includ-

ing oak, ash, maple, poplar, and pine.

The primary difference between handmade and factory-made safes is found in the panels. Mass-produced safes can usually be identified by their relatively simple pierced decorations of flower, star, or geometric patterns. Moreover, every tin in the safe is identical: if the panels were removed and stacked on top of one another, the holes in all the tins would line up perfectly.

In handmade safes, each panel is slightly different. Made from a sheet of tin or a flattened food can, panels show folk images of birds, people, ships, flags, flowers, and almost anything else that the maker could punch out with a hammer and nail.

While the pierced panels are the most important basis for determining the value of handmade safes (which command significantly higher prices than mass-produced safes), other factors also affect the worth of antique pieces. When a food safe was fabricated from cheaper woods, such as pine and poplar, it was usually painted, sometimes with graining, to hide its humble origins. Collectors prize pieces with an original coat of red, blue, green, or yellow paint. Less desirable are safes painted gray, white, or black. Unpainted safes made of fine woods like cherry and walnut, which gain a particularly handsome patina with age, are also highly valued.

Splashboards, such as the one atop the single-drawer walnut pie safe above left, made between 1830 and 1860, are typical of country pieces made in the Empire style. The worn areas on the door frames of this particular safe indicate that the surface is old. Such paint finishes, however, can be faked, and it takes a practiced eye to recognize it. The three-drawer cherry-and-poplar safe above right is from Carter County, Tennessee, and dates between 1840 and 1880.

Open Storage

In the remodeled kitchen at right, an antique plate-drying rack and a 19th-century dry sink (commonly used before kitchens had plumbing) provide open storage. A bowl of water would originally have been kept in the basin of the dry sink, with water buckets stored on the shelf below.

A country kitchen lends itself easily to open storage: there is something casual and friendly about keeping objects exposed to view rather than hiding them away behind cupboard doors.

The owner of the remodeled kitchen opposite used antique furnishings instead of shelves to hold kitchenware. The hanging rack, originally intended for drying plates, is now used to keep dinnerware close at hand. The pine dry sink underneath holds flatware, mixing bowls, and other cooking paraphernalia, and also serves as a convenient buffet when guests are expected.

In the contemporary country kitchen above, the owners opted for simple built-in shelves to store china, pottery, and glassware. Tucked below are wooden racks for spices and knives. Other items, such as seltzer bottles, vinegars, and books, are kept tidily in wire baskets on the hardwood counters.

The blue-painted worktable above holds bottles and table linens and doubles as a showcase for the homeowner's collection of spongeware.

Baskets and Bins

Tucked into the custom-built compartments above, new storage baskets with a country look are not only pretty, but practical.

Imaginative storage distinguishes these two country kitchens. In the California kitchen opposite, the homeowners had a storage island designed with a turn-of-the-century look to tie in with the decor of their 1908 house. It features glass-front bins reminiscent of those found in early-20th-century dry goods stores. The bins pull out to give easy access to the flour, rice, coffee, dried peas, pancake mix, and sugar inside. The cupboards on both sides of the stove were also designed with specialized built-ins, including a spice drawer, and other drawers for linens and utensils. All the cabinetry in the room is made of oak that has been "distressed" to look old.

The owners of the kitchen above devised innovative "drawers" by placing baskets under a counter to store potatoes, onions, and other root vegetables that need no refrigeration. Fabric liners keep the produce out of sight and can be removed for washing; handles make the baskets easy to slide in and out.

The unusual storage island in the remodeled kitchen opposite recalls an early dry goods counter. Topped with butcher block, it contains pull-out bins that can easily be cleaned with a vacuum. The small sink is used to wash vegetables.

Country Counters

Easy to maintain, plastic laminate like that used for the cheery red countertop in the kitchen at right mixes well with natural materials such as brick and wood.

ounters may indeed be the most service-able surfaces in your kitchen. And while they must withstand the wear of constant use and cleaning, they can be decorative as well.

The red laminate used in the kitchen opposite, for instance, does much to brighten up the rustic room, dominated by brick and wood. Available in a broad selection of colors and patterns suited to a country decor, plastic laminate is a preferred countertop material because it is easy to keep clean and is relatively inexpensive.

Another good choice is a solid hardwood counter like that at top left. Practical and attractive, such counters, which are generally made from durable woods like maple or oak, are best sealed with oil or polyurethane to protect them from water marks and stains.

Stone, too, makes a beautiful, long-lasting counter surface that is both heat and water resistant. The marble counter, center left, is an elegant complement to a backsplash of delicately patterned tiles.

Ceramic tiles, bottom left, also hold up well to heat and moisture, and come in ready-made and custom designs. This counter shows a classic checkerboard pattern made from standard stock-size pieces.

Among the many counter materials that can give your kitchen a country look are wood; marble; and tile, which can be used to make an effective checkerboard pattern.

STYLISH COUNTRY TILES

Ceramic tiles have been used decoratively in America since pre-Revolutionary days, when prosperous homeowners imported them from Europe to enhance the fronts of their fireplaces. Tiles did not really catch on in this country until the 1880s, but by the turn of the century they had become so popular that there were more than a hundred manufacturers making tiles for fireplaces and mantels, stoves, walls, and floors.

Although most of the early tile companies had disappeared by the 1940s, the methods for making tiles were not lost. Today tile manufacturers and craftsmen are once again producing tiles in both contemporary and revival designs.

In general, tiles come either unglazed or glazed in thicknesses ranging from ¼ to ¾ inch. In unglazed tiles, the color extends throughout the body of the clay; in glazed tiles, the color and decoration are applied to the surface of the tile. Glazed tiles are especially well suited to use on walls and backsplashes, counters, and range hoods. But because glazed tiles—particularly those with a high-gloss finish—can be slippery, they are generally not recommended for floors. When selecting tiles, be sure to tell the dealer how you intend to use them.

The decorative glazed tiles on these pages feature a few of the many designs that can work with a country-style decor. Some are stock patterns; others, such as the rabbit, rose, and blue fruit tiles, are custom-painted. While custom-made tiles can be expensive, they are an ideal way to copy a wallpaper or quilt pattern, or perhaps the design of an antique tile like one of those on the left below. Consider mixing custom or antique tiles with stock tiles to keep costs down. For additional information see page 169.

Tile Floors

Underfoot—but not out of sight—your kitchen floor is as important to the design of the room as any other element. One of the most versatile choices for covering a kitchen floor is tiling, which comes in a variety of good-looking materials and allows you to combine colors and patterns with ease.

The owner of the contemporary country kitchen opposite used twelve-inch black and white vinyl squares to create a dramatic checkerboard pattern that became the focal point of her decor. Vinyl, a resilient material that not only helps to absorb sound but is easy on the feet,

is one of the least expensive tile possibilities.

Ceramic tile, seen on the two floors above, is made from clay that has been fired at a high temperature, and it is generally somewhat more expensive than vinyl. Durable and elegant, it lends itself to many looks: solid-colored tiles, for example, can be mixed with patterned tiles as easily as with other solid hues. In the kitchen above left, an effective design was created by adding custom-made accent tiles, patterned with flowers, to a floor made of stock-size quarry tile. On the floor above right, hexagonal terracotta tiles create a striking geometric pattern.

With its natural clay color and slightly uneven surface, ceramic quarry tile, like that above left, can give a kitchen a rustic look. The simple hexagonal ceramic tiles above right create a strong design with their shapes alone.

Made of vinyl tiles, the checkerboard floor opposite is a classic country design.

SHEET VINYL FLOORING

While many of us grew up with linoleum underfoot in the kitchen, today's answer to attractive, durable, easy-to-clean flooring is sheet vinyl.

More resilient and long-lasting than linoleum (which is no longer manufactured in this country), sheet vinyl is a particularly versatile choice for a country kitchen floor. Among its many virtues are its decorative possibilities: the surprisingly broad selection of patterns includes florals, calicoes, plaids, and checks, which can lend a traditional look to a kitchen, as well as jaunty dots and graphic motifs that work well with a contemporary country decor. Still other

patterns resemble ceramic tiling or offer a convincing imitation of such natural materials as slate, wood, brick, and flagstone.

But sheet vinyl is also as practical as it is decorative. The standard stock sizes of six- and twelve-foot widths can eliminate seaming in many kitchens. And, because sheet vinyl is sold by the yard in lightweight rolls, is easy to cut, and can be laid down relatively simply, installation can be a do-it-yourself project.

Comfortable underfoot, most vinyl flooring made today has a built-in no-wax finish and requires only occasional mopping and rinsing. The samples here show just a few of the many styles available. Most patterns come in a variety of colors. See page 169 for additional information.

These sheet vinyl samples are one tenth actual size.

Painted Floors

The wood floor, above left, has been combed with a cream-colored paint: intersecting lines create a "plaid" pattern on top. A sponge-painted door jamb, above right, separates two stenciled floors.

Until well into the 19th century, most kitchens in America had bare floors. Unable to afford rugs, many people painted their wood floors to bring color and decoration to the kitchen.

Floor painting is an equally effective decorating technique in the kitchen today. It is a good way to disguise blemishes on an old surface, and it can transform any floor into a work of art. A few coats of varnish or polyurethane on top of the paint will ensure that it is long-lasting.

Among the possibilities for painting country kitchen floors are combing, sponging, stenciling, and checkerboarding. Combing, above left, involves raking a comb through a coat of wet paint to produce straight or wavy stripes. Depending on the intensity of the colors you use, you can create a very subtle effect or one of vivid contrasts.

Sponging, a technique that achieves a soft, mottled pattern, was used to decorate a door jamb, above right, and creates an effective di-

vider between the kitchen and dining area. To complete the overall design, the two different floors have been painted and stenciled in reversed colors. The homeowner based the cheerful pineapple pattern on an original stencil design by the 19th-century artist Moses Eaton, Jr.

The more intricate stencil pattern, above left, was inspired by the design on a woven coverlet that was made in the 19th century; the rust and gray hues are colors that were popular in that period. By repeating such motifs across an en-

tire floor, you can create the effect of carpeting.

Painted on a diagonal for visual interest, the green-and-white checkerboard, above right, recalls a classic pattern that was used in colonial times as an imitation of stone tiles. Here, the design was first traced with a square template, then painted on with thinned paint that allows the grain of the wood underneath to show through. A rust-colored border frames the checkerboard pattern and ties in with the cabinets, painted with the same warm shade.

The stenciled motif, above left, was based on a 19th-century coverlet pattern. Thinned paint gives the checkerboard pattern, above right, a transparent effect.

Kitchen Collectibles

trivets, molds, baskets, bowls,
beaters, grinders, mixers,
mashers, and more

As enjoyable to collect as they are to own, vintage kitchenwares make fine decorative additions to almost any country kitchen, and acquiring them can provide endless pleasure for anyone who likes exploring flea markets and antique shops. The choices can vary from yellowware and stoneware to gadgets like raisin seeders and revolving biscuit cutters, and the reasons for collecting vintage kitchenwares are as numerous as the objects themselves.

Some pieces, like brass preserving kettles or old-fashioned eggbeaters, might simply be reminders of home-cooked meals. Others, like conveyor-belt toasters, are collected as curiosities, interesting for their inventive designs. Kitchen collectibles delight, too, with their colors and patterns: decorated wares such as spatterware and spongeware are as charming today as they were when they were first introduced over a century ago. With patience and an educated eye, you can put together a fine collection of old pieces that will be a permanent reminder of the past.

Vintage storage jars, maple sugar molds, and cookie cutters make a handsome display.

Decorated Metalware

Made in the Northeast, the painted tinware above dates from the early and mid-1800s. Among the pieces on the top shelf are a coffeepot and a chocolate pot with a cone-shaped lid; and on the bottom shelf, "coffin lid" trays, canisters, and a child's cup.

A colorful and inexpensive alternative to fancier wares, decorated metalwares helped brighten the kitchens of American housewives; the detail and varied patterns of such pieces still make them appealing today.

The earliest type of painted metalware sold in this country was tinware, which first became popular in the early 1800s. A wide range of household objects like those above were shaped from tin plate (sheet iron or steel coated with tin) and then "japanned." An imitation of oriental lacquerwork, this process, which helped prevent rust, involved kiln-firing pieces that had been treated with paint pigments—usually in red, yellow, white, or black—or a dark, tar-base varnish called asphaltum. Decorators, or "flowerers," then added designs in oil colors and colored bronzes.

Graniteware, which fills the kitchen opposite, was mass-produced in America from the 1850s to the 1930s. Generally made of sheet iron or steel, this lightweight kitchenware was enameled for easy cleaning. Its swirled and speckled patterns—in blue, green, gray, red, purple, yellow, brown, or turquoise—resemble granite, which may have suggested the name of the ware.

The owners of the kitchen opposite designed the cheerful room around their collection of graniteware, which numbers more than 150 pieces. In the early 1900s such utensils sold for pennies apiece.

Copper and Tin

Cooking utensils like those made of copper, left, and tin plate, above, were used widely in America between the 17th and 19th centuries. Most copper cookware was imported from Europe until well into the 1800s; in fact, few existing American copper utensils are known to have been made before 1850. Unlike silversmiths, coppersmiths seldom marked their work, so dating is difficult.

The food molds displayed on the cookstove above are made of tin plate. Used in the colonies as early as 1700, this inexpensive and malleable material was commonly formed into molds for "fancy dishes" such as jellies, cakes, chocolate, ice cream, and puddings.

Copper cookware, like that at left, is valued for its rich luster and even heat conduction.

Among the tin molds above are some of the most commonly made shapes: chickens, eggs, hearts, and shells. The turkey and pumpkin molds were designed to make chocolate treats for Thanksgiving and Halloween.

Vintage Baking Utensils

While recipes for homemade breads, cakes, cookies, muffins, and pies—both sweet and savory—are often passed down through generations, many of the utensils once used to prepare these baked goods have been replaced by more modern alternatives.

The collection at left features baking utensils from the early 20th century. Today collectors prize such utensils, in part because they recall a simpler time when home baking was a routine household activity and an age of electric mixers and food processors was unimaginable.

Like contemporary kitchenware, however, these vintage pieces were also intended to lighten cooking tasks. Some pieces, for example, were designed to do more than one job: double-ended spoons measured teaspoons and tablespoons, and calibrated funnels also served as measuring cups.

Other utensils, like the two unusual rolling pins shown here, were simply innovative variations on a standard form. The wooden rolling pin with a double-barred handle was designed to give the baker a better grip. The hollow glass pin came fitted with a cork stopper and could be filled with ice water to keep the dough chilled and easy to work. Frequently embellished with nautical mottoes, glass rolling pins are thought to have been given as gifts by sailors to their sweethearts or mothers. Decorated with enamel, the one here is, in fact, inscribed "For my Mother."

Once prepared, the dough for cookies and biscuits was shaped with cutters, which were usually made of wood or tin in a variety of designs, including hearts, animals, stars, and birds. In addition to single cookie cutters, there were also revolving cutters, fitted with handles, which could be rolled continuously across the dough to speed cutting. Some rolling cutters could also produce multiple patterns.

An equally clever tool, used for pie making, was the crimper, or jagger, which was generally made of brass, and sometimes of horn, wood, whalebone, or tin. Consisting of a handle attached to a saw-toothed wheel, the handy device trimmed excess dough from the crusts, leaving a fancy edge, and at the same time sealed the top and bottom crusts.

Other convenient devices included ridged tin bread pans, which left an imprint on the loaf to indicate where it should be sliced, and wooden bread slicers designed with evenly spaced knife guides.

While many vintage baking utensils can still be used, collectors generally recommend reserving fragile or hard-to-clean pieces for display.

Among the early-20th-century baking utensils at left are some particularly inventive designs, including a revolving biscuit cutter and a hollow glass rolling pin that could be filled with cold water.

Hearth Utensils

Hand-forged by blacksmiths, wrought-iron utensils like the 18th-century skewers, spatulas, and fork above were often custom-made to suit a particular fireplace. While English pieces were sometimes heavily ornamented, iron utensils made in this country were almost always simple in design.

Attracted by the straightforward, handsome forms of early cooking utensils, the owner of this Texas kitchen created a striking display by silhouetting her 18th- and 19th-century pieces against walls of whitewashed pine.

These utensils are typical of the sturdy tools used for open-hearth cooking, which was common in America until the middle of the 19th century. Iron skewers like the rare examples above were used to attach meat and fowl to a roasting spit. The fork and spatulas helped spear or turn foods, their long handles allowing the cook to stand back from the heat of the fire. Among the other early tools in the collection are the 18th-century dough scrapers hung on a meat hook to the right of the stove. The unusual iron piece to the left of them is a weather vane that came from a Pennsylvania barn.

The collection of utensils in this kitchen includes the spoons and skimmers over the sink, right. These date from the mid-1700s to the early 1800s.

COOKING AT THE HEARTH

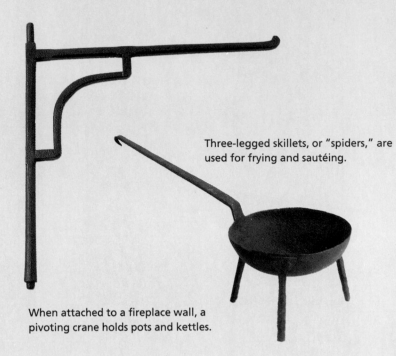

Three-legged skillets, or "spiders," are used for frying and sautéing.

When attached to a fireplace wall, a pivoting crane holds pots and kettles.

With long-handled tools, the "hearther" can turn, baste, skim, and ladle food while standing back from the coals.

A shovel is used to move hot coals from the fire to the front of the hearth.

A reflector oven, or "tin kitchen," is used on the hearth.

Before the advent of wood-burning cookstoves in the 1850s, most meals were prepared at the fireplace. Open-hearth cooking was a time-consuming process, but one so central to domestic life that Harriet Beecher Stowe once wrote, "An open fire is the altar of patriotism. Would our Revolutionary fathers have gone barefooted and bleeding over snows to defend air-tight stoves. . .? I trow not."

Today, as interest in early American life grows, hearth cookery is undergoing a revival. Many individuals, historical societies, and museums now offer classes in the technique, and serious "hearthers" are forming groups to share advice and recipes.

If you want to try hearth cookery, which can be done in any standard fireplace, you will need some durable cookware like the iron pieces shown on these pages. While antiques are available, you can also purchase less expensive reproduction ironware made by contemporary artisans.

Among the choices are pieces that are actually hung inside the fireplace, such as pots and kettles, as well as trivets and footed skillets that are usually used to cook "down hearth" —or outside the fireplace on the hearth itself. Long-handled utensils, such as spatulas, forks, spoons, and skimmers, are also essential.

Once you are equipped with the right cookware, you will find that a surprisingly wide range of dishes can be prepared at the hearth, including soups, stews, meats and poultry, breads, cakes, and pies. Cookbooks offering historical and contemporary recipes for this satisfying method of cooking are available.

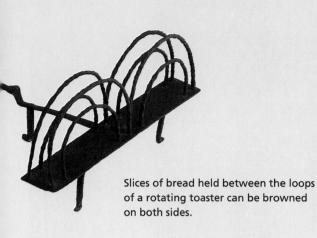

Slices of bread held between the loops of a rotating toaster can be browned on both sides.

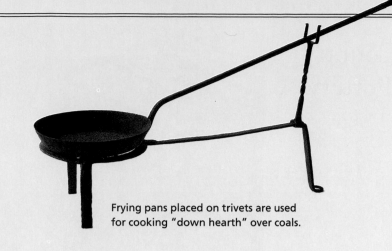

Frying pans placed on trivets are used for cooking "down hearth" over coals.

Hung from a crane or set on a stand, a tea kettle can keep hot water on hand.

A trivet, or gridiron, holds cookware near the fire or serves as a broiler.

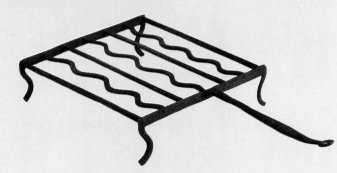

A rotary broiler can be turned in front of the coals on the hearth to cook meat and poultry evenly.

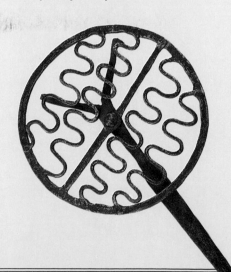

Kettles and pots (preferably with lids to keep out ashes) can be used for simmering soups, vegetables, and stews.

Country Pottery

Made around the turn of the century, blue-and-white stoneware like that at right was originally given away as a premium by Sears, Roebuck and Company. It was decorated in hundreds of embossed patterns, including flowers, fruits, animals, Dutch scenes, and Indian heads, and is a sought-after collectible today.

From the 17th century onward, abundant clay deposits in England and America supplied the raw material for a broad range of ceramic kitchenware. Among the many types of pottery that were both imported and made domestically were stoneware, mochaware, and redware.

Blue-and-white stoneware like that opposite was made primarily from the turn of the century until the late 1930s. Mass-produced, this inexpensive molded pottery included pitchers, bowls, crocks, and jugs and was often decorated with embossed designs, decals, or stencils.

Colorful mochaware, above left, takes its name from a type of agate called mocha stone: the decorations on this earthenware resemble the mosslike brown, black, green, or red markings in the rock. Mochaware was made in England from the late 1700s to the mid-1800s and was imported to America as "poor man's china." Its vivid decorative motifs bear such fanciful names as cat's eye, earthworm, and seaweed.

Redware, above right, made from the coarse clay found in plentiful supply along the Atlantic seaboard, was the first pottery to be produced in the colonies. Hand-thrown and coated with a clear lead glaze to render them waterproof, redware pieces include crocks, plates, jugs, mugs, and bowls. The yellow decoration commonly found on this ware is a liquid clay, called slip, which was trailed over the glaze from a special cup fitted with a hollow turkey quill.

The collection of English mochaware above left includes mugs and pitchers, two of the more commonly found forms of this pottery. The redware above right probably dates from the 1800s. Because antique redware has a lead glaze, it should not be used for serving food.

Yellowware

One of the most popular utility potteries of the late 1800s and early 1900s was yellowware, which is displayed in the pantry at left and in the 19th-century cupboard above.

Produced primarily in New Jersey and Ohio from local clay that fired to a dull yellow, the durable ceramic was used for all manner of kitchen utensils. It was particularly suitable for bakeware because it could withstand high temperatures. The earliest examples were hand-thrown on a potter's wheel; later pieces were cast in molds. Decoration usually consisted of blue, brown, or white bands, although solid-color wares sometimes had embossed patterns.

The 19th-century yellowware in the Minnesota
pantry at left still stands up well to use today.

Among the most common forms of yellowware were mixing bowls like the 19th-century pieces above, which were often decorated with three white bands. The two molds on the top shelf are for cakes and corn bread; such pieces were typically embossed with corn or other symbols of plenty.

This American pitcher features the "chickenwire" design in blue and white, the most valued of two-color combinations.

Butter tubs with stenciled lettering, like this one, are prized by collectors.

Porringer cups like this example were used for serving porridge or gruel.

BUTTER

SPONGEWARE

Spongeware has captured the hearts of American collectors, yet almost every piece is an object of mystery. Many questions about this mottled pottery can never be answered because few pieces were marked by their makers.

We do know that spongeware originated in England in the late 18th century and was adopted by American potters sometime after 1830. Most of what is found on the market today, however, was not made until after the turn of the 19th century.

"Spongeware" refers to any piece of pottery whose decoration was dabbed on with a sponge or another soft material. While the mottled patterns appear on many types of pottery bodies, including stoneware, yellowware, and redware, they most often occur on utilitarian, rather than decorative, pieces. As a rule, American spongeware is found in blue and white, green and white, and tricolored patterns of brown, green, and ocher. English pieces tend to be colored with blue and white or a mix of blue, green, and red.

Although spongeware was not made with particular patterns in mind, collectors have now assigned names to some of the more common sponged designs. "Smoke ring," for example, comprises large, irregularly shaped circles; "chickenwire" refers to smaller connecting rings. Shown here are a few of the many types of pieces available to collectors.

The tricolored decoration on this bean pot makes it more valuable than the more common two-color pieces.

Spongeware platters and creamers like those above are both rare and desirable. The small mug, left, is probably English.

Depression Collectibles

Kitchen utensils made from the 1920s through the 1940s are among the most affordable collectibles, and can bring a casual, nostalgic look to a country kitchen.

The owner of the 1940s kitchen at left used existing cubby shelves to display a collection of canteens and water pitchers made by Universal Potteries of Ohio in the 1930s and 1940s. Universal pottery was often decorated with decals and came in matched sets, which included both table and cook wares. The period look of these pieces is echoed by the Depression-glass juicers hung by the window.

Other Depression-glass pieces are displayed above. Once given away as premiums in soap boxes and at movie theaters, this inexpensive, machine-made glassware was produced in more than a hundred patterns.

Depression glass like that above ranged from fancy stemmed goblets to everyday butter dishes, and was made in such colors as cobalt blue, green, amber, pink, and amethyst. Patterns bore romantic names, like "American Sweetheart," "Royal Lace," and "Princess."

The water servers at left were made by Universal Potteries in the 1930s and 1940s. Among the decal patterns are "Calico Fruit" and "Kitchen Bouquet."

Toast's Up

The electric toaster was first patented in 1906 and has been serving up toast ever since. But toasters haven't always popped: they also swung, rotated, pinched, and even flopped the bread. Now these old machines—with their whimsical shapes and complex mechanisms—have become collector's items.

Vintage toasters that still operate are a find, but even if they don't work, their ingenious designs can be fascinating. Consider the Toast-O-Lator, for example, which carries the toast past hot coils on a conveyor belt and even has a peephole; or, the early toaster oven, complete with warmers for rolls and coffeepot. Luckily for anyone who wants to begin a collection, old toasters can be found at flea markets and antique shops. In particular, collectors value those with toast racks and push buttons, as well as pieces made with porcelain.

1. Drop-down toaster with blue lacquer sides, c. 1940. 2. Toast-O-Lator conveyor belt toaster, c. 1941. 3. Simplex model toaster with warming rack, c. 1914. 4. Early toaster oven, c. 1937. 5. Swing-basket toaster with push buttons, c. 1929. 6. Four-slice, "family-size" swing toaster, c. 1925. 7. Nickel-plated toaster with automatic pop-out carrier and dark/light temperature lever, c. 1925. 8. Early percher toaster (one of the first electric models), with porcelain base, c. 1909.

Antique Wooden-ware

The simple beauty, texture, and hand-craftsmanship that characterize antique woodenware make it a natural complement to the country kitchen.

Found in plentiful supply, wood was the most essential raw material available to the early colonists, who used it to make virtually every type of kitchenware. Known as treen (meaning "made of tree"), wooden objects for preparing, serving, and storing food were turned out by village coopers and by settlers making their own home furnishings.

Woodenware was made and extensively used—especially by rural folk and settlers migrating westward—until the 19th century, when factory-made pottery and metalware became more widely available. Pieces were generally shaped with hand tools or turned on a lathe; some, like the 19th-century New England bowls above, were often protected and brightened with homemade paints, usually brown, blue, red, gray, or yellow.

The 19th-century bucket bench opposite holds wooden pieces that would have been common in kitchens of the 1700s and 1800s. The green-painted box, for example, once contained salt, which was used for preserving as well as flavoring foods. To keep the salt from absorbing moisture, such boxes were customarily hung in a warm, dry spot near a fireplace.

Continued

In addition to woodenware, baskets were among the most useful and versatile household items in early America. Used for drying, gathering, carrying, and storing food, the baskets on the bucket bench at left were all made in the 1800s.

Among the pieces of antique woodenware in the collection above are plates and larger platters, paddles, and scoops. The 18th-century butter print on the top shelf has a carved thistle pattern. Such prints, which were both hand-carved and factory-made, are also found in oblong and square shapes and in many other patterns, including birds and animals.

Other, longer boxes were generally used to store cutlery or hand-dipped tallow candles.

Among the most common types of kitchenware were large shallow bowls, which were used as basins for chopping food or as communal eating vessels from which diners served themselves using smaller bowls, wooden spoons, or their fingers. Other wares included wooden plates, as well as larger platters like those above known as trenchers (the term "trencher" may derive from a definition of the Old French verb *trenchier,* meaning "to carve"). It was considered thrifty for two people to eat from the same trencher, and when courting couples did so they were deemed engaged.

Although one side of the plate or trencher was usually rimmed, both sides were actually used to serve food: after the main part of the meal had been eaten on the "dinner side," the plate was

flipped over to the "pie side" for the next course.

The plates shown here are primarily made of maple, a dense, satiny hardwood that was often used for kitchenware. The trencher second from left on the bottom shelf is of curly maple. Prized by the colonists for its distinctive wavy grain, pieces made of this wood are valued among collectors today.

Most of the other pieces on the shelves were used for preparing butter. After the cream "broke" in the churn, the buttermilk was drained off and the remaining substance was washed and salted. The mixture was then turned out and pressed with paddles, called butter workers, to remove the liquid. A carved butter print might then be used to imprint a butter maker's trademark before the product was brought to market. Butter made at home was also stamped, but purely for decoration.

CARING FOR WOODENWARE

Woodenware, like any valued collectible, requires special care. After you buy an old wooden piece, the first step is to check it for insects. Set the piece on a sheet of black paper and leave it undisturbed for a week. If small, sand-colored "grains" appear, place the object in a plastic bag with a few mothballs or a bug-repellent vapor strip, and seal the bag tightly. As an immediate measure, this will protect your house from infestation, but you will still need to take the item to a professional for thorough fumigating. (Once treated for insects, a piece should never touch food.)

If your woodenware is not fragile it can be cleaned at home: dust gently with a small, dry bristle brush, or use a sponge slightly dampened with a weak solution made of warm water and an oil-base soap formulated for wood. Never soak wood or leave it under running water. Let the piece dry slowly, away from direct light and heat, to prevent warping.

Woodenware should be kept free of dust, which attracts damaging moisture. Pieces that are "finished" (this term refers to a natural burnish that comes with years of use) can be coated lightly with beeswax or a microcrystalline wax to keep them free of dust. Be sure not to use vegetable, mineral, or linseed oil, floor wax, furniture polish, or any other sticky substance on woodenware. Pieces that have an "unfinished," or dry, matte surface should be left alone.

Store and display your woodenware in a cool, ventilated, relatively dust- and grease-free environment. Keeping pieces in a dark, damp place can cause mildew, and putting them in a hot, dry area may result in cracks.

Woodenware should also be used carefully. Because wood absorbs and retains oils and other substances that could be toxic, and because it is difficult to clean thoroughly, it is best not to let old pieces come into direct contact with food. Moreover, placing food in an antique piece can permanently stain the wood. Experts advise that it is better to reserve antique woodenware for display only, although it is probably safe to use pieces for serving dry foods such as crackers or breads. If you do, you should use a glass or cloth liner, as this will protect both the food and the piece itself.

Homespun Touches

The gingham garments above include bonnets and aprons from Ohio and Pennsylvania. These homespun pieces are typical of the work clothes worn by 19th-century farm wives.

Homespun fabrics were as much a part of the early American woman's domestic life as pots and pans. And today they add warmth to any country kitchen.

The owner of the homespun pieces above collects them because they remind her of her mother, who "lived in an apron" on the family farm. These bonnets and aprons date from the late 1800s. In the simple kitchen at right, a Shaker peg rack displays similar garments, which came from Iowa. The checked napkins are made from homespun scraps.

The owner of the kitchen at right collects homespun for its soft, "used" look.

COLLECTIBLE RECIPE BOOKS

A delight to anyone interested in the history of cooking, in illustration, or simply in food itself, the recipe pamphlets and cookbooks saved by generations of American housewives are fascinating mementos of our culinary heritage.

Many of the books and pamphlets at left were produced by food and appliance companies as premiums and giveaways to promote a particular product. Often a great deal of money was put into preparing these pieces, and it was not uncommon for companies to hire such famous artists as Maxfield Parrish and Norman Rockwell to illustrate them.

While many collectors prize early recipe books for their graphics, others enjoy them simply because they are amusing. Who can resist a 1923 cookbook entitled *The Motorist's Luncheon Book,* which offers recipes for toasted herring (cooked over hot coals) and spaghetti rarebit (made in a chafing dish outdoors)? What fun to own a pamphlet called *Favorite Recipes for Country Kitchens,* produced by General Foods in 1945, with recipes for hamburger shortcake, daffodil orange cake, and creamed eggs on cheese squares.

Vintage pieces such as these only grow more valuable over time. Think twice before you throw away the recipe books and pamphlets you receive today; they will undoubtedly be tomorrow's collectibles.

The Pantry

*a convenient place for storing
and displaying your
kitchen goods*

To most people, a traditional pantry means a cool, dark room near the kitchen, a room stocked with fresh foods and canned goods and filled with the scents of herbs and spices. Before home refrigeration became common in the late 1800s, this versatile storage and work room—usually fitted with a stone or wood sink—could be found in most homes. Shelves held seasonings, meal, and sugar; dairy products were kept cool on a stone or dirt floor.

Today, many homeowners don't have the space in their houses to devote a whole room to pantry storage. But, with a little imagination, it is still possible to create the effect of a pantry in almost any kitchen. You might try using an old pie safe to store kitchenware. Or, fill a wall of open shelving with jars of preserves. Even tabletops and corners can evoke a pantry feeling when set up to dry herbs and vegetables or to store wares and utensils. The ideas that follow should convince you that there is always room for a pantry in a country kitchen.

Tin-lidded jars and glazed pottery line the shelves of a Maryland pantry.

117

Traditional Pantries

Food safes, such as the red-painted Ohio piece above left, made around 1870, were commonly used in American kitchens in the 19th and early 20th centuries. Jelly cupboards, like the one above right, are still useful for storing preserves today.

Whether used to store food, tableware, or cookware, country pantries can be as large as a room—or as small as a piece of furniture.

During the 18th and 19th centuries, for example, produce, meat, and baked goods were commonly kept in food safes, which were often placed on a cool back porch or in the cellar. The 19th-century safe above left was built with a screened door to admit fresh air while protecting food from insects and rodents. Its slatted shelves enhance air circulation. Jelly cupboards, like the one above right, were often shallower than food safes and were fitted with narrower shelves that could hold a row or two of preserve jars.

The walk-in pantry opposite, located in a suburban Ohio house, re-creates the look of a traditional farmhouse pantry, which usually had shelves on three sides and at least one window for light and ventilation. Used to store food, this pantry also serves as a display space for a collection of yellowware and stoneware.

In the traditional walk-in pantry opposite, dried flowers hang from beams, stoneware crocks and yellowware bowls are organized on wide shelves, and fresh garden produce is kept cool on the floor. A toolbox serves as a handy berry basket.

An Amish Pantry

The fruits of an abundant harvest fill the shelves of the whitewashed canning cellar above, which has been fully stocked by an Amish family in Lancaster County, Pennsylvania. A religious congregation committed to a disciplined life that centers on church, family, and farm, the Amish sect was founded in Europe in 1693. Members continue to live self-sufficiently in a number of rural areas around America.

Growing produce is a traditional household activity among the Amish, and preserving occupies a large part of the Amish woman's time.

She cans fruits and vegetables in summer and preserves various kinds of meats in winter. Pantries such as this one are customarily stocked with enough jams, jellies, conserves, and pickled vegetables to feed family, guests, and harvesting crews.

Some Amish pantries might contain as many as a thousand quarts of provisions "put by" at the end of a growing season. The recycling of food jars is common among these thrifty people, and it is not unusual to find jars in an Amish pantry that have been used for forty or fifty years.

The Amish pantry at left is filled with preserved goods made from recipes that are passed down from mother to daughter. These foods are considered by the Amish to be as beneficial for the soul as they are for the body.

GIFTS FROM THE PANTRY

Putting food by to give as gifts is a country tradition of long standing. After enough preserves were made for the family's use, a portion of any batch was almost always earmarked for friends.

The recipes here are quick and easy to prepare—all take under an hour. The relish and conserve are made in relatively small quantities in jars with clamped glass lids. The jars are processed (immersed in boiling water and vacuum sealed) using a large cooking pot and a wire rack.

The Corn-Cabbage Relish is a variation on the Pennsylvania German "seven sweets and seven sours" traditionally served with every festive meal. The Three-Fruit Conserve makes an unusual condiment to serve with roasted meat or poultry, and it is also delicious as a dessert, topped with vanilla ice cream. And while the Sweet and Spicy Nuts can be addicting, they are easy to replenish.

Sweet and Spicy Nuts go particularly well with a glass of dry sherry before dinner, or with afternoon tea.

SWEET AND SPICY NUTS

1 egg white, lightly beaten	1 teaspoon salt
2 tablespoons soy sauce	1 teaspoon ground cumin
1 tablespoon Worcestershire sauce	½ teaspoon black pepper
1 tablespoon corn oil	¼ teaspoon cayenne pepper
3 garlic cloves, minced	½ pound pecan halves
¼ cup sugar	½ pound whole almonds

1. Preheat the oven to 350°. Line 2 baking sheets with foil.

2. In a shallow bowl, combine the egg white, soy and Worcestershire sauces, oil, garlic, 3 tablespoons of the sugar, ½ teaspoon of the salt, ½ teaspoon of the cumin, ¼ teaspoon of the black pepper, and ⅛ teaspoon of the cayenne and stir until well blended; set aside.

3. In a medium-size saucepan of boiling water, blanch the pecans and almonds for 1 minute. Drain and immediately dredge them in the egg white mixture.

4. With a slotted spoon, spread the nuts on the baking sheets, separating them if they clump together. Bake the nuts for 15 minutes.

5. Reduce the oven temperature to 325°, stir the nuts, and bake for 20 to 30 minutes more, or until crisp and golden, stirring occasionally to ensure even browning.

6. Meanwhile, in a shallow bowl, combine the remaining 1 tablespoon sugar, ½ teaspoon salt, ½ teaspoon cumin, ¼ teaspoon black pepper, and ⅛ teaspoon cayenne. When the nuts are done, remove them from the oven and dredge them in the sugar-spice mixture while they're still hot. Set aside to cool and then store in an airtight container for up to 3 weeks.

Makes about 4 cups

CORN-CABBAGE RELISH

7 cups corn kernels, fresh or frozen	1 cup finely chopped cabbage
1 red bell pepper, coarsely chopped	1½ cups sugar
	2 tablespoons salt
1 green bell pepper, coarsely chopped	2 teaspoons celery seed
	2 teaspoons mustard seed
1 large yellow onion, coarsely chopped	⅛ teaspoon black pepper
	2 cups white vinegar

1. In a large nonreactive saucepan, place the corn, bell peppers, onion, cabbage, sugar, salt, celery and mustard seeds, pepper, vinegar, and 2 cups of water. Bring to a boil over medium-high heat and cook, partially covered, until the relish has thickened, about 20 minutes.

2. Pack the relish into 6 hot sterilized pint jars to within ½ inch of the rim. Wipe the rims and seal the jars. Lower the jars onto a rack in a large pot of boiling water. The tops should be covered by 1 to 2 inches of water and the jars should not touch one another. Return to a boil and process the jars for 15 minutes. Store in a cool, dark place for at least 6 weeks before serving.

Makes 6 pints

THREE-FRUIT CONSERVE

6 peaches (about 2½ pounds)
6 pears (3½ to 4 pounds)
6 plums (about 1¼ pounds)
2 quarts cider vinegar

4 cups granulated sugar
2 cups (packed) dark brown sugar
Seven 4-inch cinnamon sticks
Grated zest of 1 lemon

1. Peel, halve, and pit peaches, pears, and plums. In a large nonreactive saucepan, bring the vinegar, 4 cups of water, the granulated and dark brown sugars, cinnamon sticks, and lemon zest to a boil over medium-high heat. Cover the pan, reduce the heat to medium-low, and simmer for 15 minutes. Return to a boil over high heat.

2. Add the fruit to the saucepan, reduce the heat to low, and simmer until the fruit is just tender, about 5 minutes.

3. With a slotted spoon, transfer the fruit to 7 hot sterilized pint jars and fill to within ½ inch of the rim. Remove the cinnamon sticks from the poaching syrup and set aside. Pour the syrup into the jars. Run a table knife around the inside of the jars to remove any air bubbles, then insert 1 of the reserved cinnamon sticks into each jar. Wipe the rims and seal the jars.

4. Lower the jars onto a rack in a large pot of boiling water. The tops should be covered by 1 to 2 inches of water and the jars should not touch one another. Return to a boil and process the jars for 15 minutes. Store in a cool, dark place for at least 4 weeks before serving.

Makes 7 pints

The Three-Fruit Conserve and the Corn-Cabbage Relish, above, make good gifts at any time of year. Both may be put up in either pint or quart jars.

Space-Saving Pantries

For homeowners who do not have an extra room for a full pantry, a wall of shelves or a pull-out cabinet can make an efficient, space-saving alternative. The narrow floor-to-ceiling "shelf pantry" in the Connecticut kitchen at left, for example, takes advantage of what might have been empty wall space to store jars of the owner's homemade preserves and condiments.

In the contemporary California kitchen above, the sliding pantry, designed as a vertical drawer, brings foodstuffs within easy reach. The shallow shelves are accessible from both sides.

The simple, Shaker-style wall shelving at left stores preserves made mainly for gift giving.

No space is wasted with the pull-out pantry above, which keeps canned and dried goods organized on thirteen-inch-wide shelves.

Pantry Options

The improvised pantry above was created with an arrangement of glass jars and an antique workbench. Woven place mats and jars of preserves are tucked neatly on the lower shelf.

With imagination and a bit of handi-work, you can create a pantry in almost no space at all using simple materials. Building a few shelves into a closet, for example, will produce a serviceable pantry for stocking food and cookware. And even a collection of glass containers set on a bench or tabletop becomes a pantry if need be.

On the "workbench pantry" above, vintage jars were put to use holding dried peas, lentils, nuts, flowers, and bouquets garnis. The colorful contents of the jars turn a plain piece of furniture into an attractive showcase.

The well-organized storeroom at right, part of a recently built Long Island country house, was designed with beaded-board walls for a turn-of-the-century look and fitted with floor-to-ceiling shelves mounted on simple brackets. The two-drawer chest under the window is a traditional pantry feature, used to store table linens.

Beaded-board paneling, simple bracketed shelves, and cotton curtains give the pantry at left a refreshing country feeling. The entire space was painted white for a clean, light effect.

Fancy ribbons and beautiful bows, hand-lettered labels and fabric lid covers—these are the simple but special touches that can bring color to your pantry or kitchen shelves and turn preserved foods into attractive gifts.

Whether your preserves are homemade or store-bought, pretty labels will dress them up and make them easy to find on the shelves. Purchase plain or decorative adhesive la-

bels or make your own from construction paper. Hand-letter the labels to indicate the contents of your jars and bottles and add a message if you plan to give them as gifts. You can use rubber stamps and colorful inks to decorate the labels with such country motifs as stars, teddy bears, roosters, hearts, cows, or crescent moons. Affix the labels with rubber cement if they are not preglued.

As an alternative to labels, con-

sider cutting out heart-shaped patterns or other simple designs from fabric or paper and gluing them to the jar or bottle.

Caps made from fabric swatches or paper in plain colors, ginghams, plaids, or small prints will also give your jars an appealing country look. To make them, cut circles or squares at least two inches bigger than the jar lid and scallop the edges with scissors or trim with pinking shears.

To center the cap properly and to keep it from slipping, anchor it to the jar lid with a small piece of double-sided tape, then fold down the sides and further secure with a rubber band just below the rim of the lid. Once the cap is in place, gather it to create a skirted effect. Conceal the rubber band with a pretty ribbon, fabric trimming, or with a piece of twine, and add colorful paper cutouts or small ornaments, if desired.

Dressed-up jars and bottles will add country flavor to your pantry or kitchen shelves. The decorations shown here include paper and fabric caps, ribbon ties, and hand-lettered labels.

The Butler's Pantry

*Mini-print wallpaper,
framed botanical prints, and
grain-painted cabinetry
bring country-style elegance
to the butler's pantry
at right.*

The butler's pantry, which originated as a service room between the kitchen and dining room in the early 1800s, still has a place in the country home today. The pantry at left is a classic example, incorporating glass-front cabinets to store dinnerware, specialized drawers for linens and cutlery, and a sink.

Suited to relaxed country living, the wet bar in a corner of the kitchen above functions as a compact, modern-day version of the traditional butler's pantry. Goblets, glasses, and tumblers are stored neatly in a custom-made cupboard above the sink. A latticelike rack keeps wine bottles at the proper angle.

Above, a wet bar—a small, simplified version of the butler's pantry—combines open shelving, glass-front cabinetry, and a convenient wine rack.

Pantry
in a
Corner

At right, an old table
transforms a corner into a
pantry for storing preserves
and stoneware. The tall
"twigs" in the basket next
to the table are
cinnamon sticks.

132

You can achieve the feeling of a country pantry in your kitchen simply by transforming an unused corner with a rustic table, old kitchenware, and some fresh, canned, or dried garden produce.

The corner pantry opposite, for instance, was created at one end of a small passageway located off the kitchen. Here, an old worktable holds stoneware and homemade preserves. A wire basket filled with cookie cutters, and a collection of wooden utensils, including butter paddles, ladles, pestles, and a ribbed rolling pin, hang from the overhead shelf.

The pantry in the corner above receives plenty of morning sunshine and is an ideal place for drying chilies. After picking the red and green peppers, the homeowners string them on twine and hang them for at least two weeks or until they are brittle. In addition to brightening the space with their color, the chilies can be removed as needed and used in cooking. (Eventually stored in tightly lidded jars, the dried chili peppers will hold their heat and flavor for up to two years.) The dried herbs hanging beside the chilies are also ready for use, and fill the small space with their fragrance.

In the corner above, chilies dry in the sunlight. A cluster of pitchers, crocks, bowls, and jugs completes the simple pantry arrangement.

Country Table Settings

ideas for presenting your meals with style

Setting a country table is an easy way to decorate on a small scale. Whether you plan ahead of time or improvise, your country table setting can reflect the season, the latest color trend, a special occasion, or your own whim. It is simplest to work with whatever tablewares and linens you have on hand; the only "rule" is to arrange them with imagination.

You might, for example, try using ordinary items in new ways: seashells can stand in for salt and pepper shakers, or a watering can might become a vase. Or, you can combine the unexpected: pair silver forks with enamel spoons, or flea-market pottery with heirloom china. You don't even need a dining table—spreading out a blanket for a fireside picnic, setting individual trays, or presenting a buffet for a party are all equally appealing ideas for serving a country meal.

Yellowware arranged on a homespun cloth makes a simple country table setting.

Simple
Is
Beautiful

Antique treenware—including a plate and breadboards that date from the 1800s—enhances the country look of the table above.

Some of the most attractive table settings are the simplest. Even a plain wooden table needs few adornments: left bare of a cloth or place mats, it can make a beautiful backdrop for country dining.

Set with antique china and enamelware, the 19th-century pine table at right is ready for a stoveside breakfast. At this informal meal, the cookware is also used for serving. Diners can help themselves directly from the iron skillets and the graniteware coffeepot on the stove.

Enhanced by the scrubbed pine table and woodenware above, the ingredients of a casual country lunch—bread, Brie, Red Bartlett pears—become as important to the setting as the tableware. When filled with fruit, a wooden bowl makes a pretty centerpiece.

Flow Blue china, known for its slightly blurred underglaze, suits the rustic setting at right.

Mix and Match

Friendly and inviting, these two table settings express the casual character of country style with combinations of different patterns and materials related by a theme.

A blue-and-white color scheme unifies the cheerful setting opposite, in which unmatched pottery and linens are used together. A plaid tablecloth is teamed with napkins in a complementary check, while new homespun hearts—Christmas-tree ornaments that serve as a centerpiece during the rest of the year—add their own patterns to the table. Reproduction pewter service plates set off the spatterware dishes.

On the table above, a heart motif, which appears on the spongeware plate and in the shapes of the iron trivet handle and candle holders, creates a harmonizing theme for the eclectic selection of country tableware. Sewn into a place mat, patchwork pieces make a colorful background for a red plaid napkin and antique flatware in two different patterns.

The place setting above displays a clever mix of household items put to use as table decor. Tin candy molds serve as holders for votive candles, and a dishtowel has been folded as a napkin.

Splashes of vivid red complement the blue-and-white color scheme of the table setting opposite: a red place mat anchors the centerpieces, and a bowl of raw cranberries makes an original table decoration.

A History of Flatware

When Americans sit down at the dining table and pick up a fork, knife, or spoon, few probably realize that the present-day customs for eating with these utensils date back only a few hundred years.

In fact, the table fork did not evolve until the late 1500s. While forks existed then, they were used mainly for serving; it was the hunting knife, the spoon, and fingers that brought food to mouth. During the 1600s, however, the fork caught on as an eating utensil. Individuals considered their forks personal belongings and often took them along when they dined away from home.

While the earliest forks were small, two-pronged devices, it is impossible to date a fork simply by its size or the number of tines. By the 1700s, for example, table forks with three and four tines were available, yet two-tined examples continued to be made as late as the Victorian era.

Knives have an equally interesting history. The first table knives, which appeared around 1600, usually had a tapered blade with a sharp point, and food was eaten right off the tip. When the table fork became the preferred eating utensil, the knife blade became wider, with a rounded end, and was used for cutting and spreading. Early knife handles were made of wood or bone; silver, porcelain, and earthenware became popular materials in the 1700s. During the 1800s, ivory, horn, and mother-of-pearl were fashionable.

Spoons, too, have had a distinctive evolution. Medieval spoons were usually made of horn, wood, or tin. By the 1600s, pewter and brass were common, while silver was reserved for fine flatware. Most metal spoons made before the mid-1700s had a fig- or ellipse-shaped bowl; those made later often had narrow, oval bowls.

Although today flatware is made in a seemingly endless range of styles, the designs often find their inspiration in the past. The pistol-grip handle, for instance, originated almost three hundred years ago as a sheath to protect folding knives and forks, yet it is still a popular handle form. Classic 18th-century patterns like the scallop shell are also being reproduced, and traditional techniques such as hand hammering are being applied to new silver. The flatware shown here reveals distinctive designs, both old and new. See page 169 for more information.

The flatware at right includes pieces as old as a 17th-century beaded fork and knife and as recent as a 1980s set of utensils with red ceramic handles. Other interesting pieces include a matching two-pronged fork and knife with stag-antler handles, c. 1820, and a fork, spoon, and knife with handles made of Bakelite, c. 1930.

Tabletop Surprises

The table decor above works because each element—from the patterned dishware to the thick-stemmed wine glasses and stainless-steel flatware—makes its own strong visual statement.

A creative setting can often be achieved by introducing objects that are not customarily found on a dining table, or by combining traditional pieces in an inventive way.

The focal point of the tabletop design above is the simple but surprising centerpiece: a green-painted toolbox planted with golden narcissus. The carefree feeling of the flowers is echoed in the patterns of the unmatched Portuguese ceramic plates and in the windowpane-check tea towels used as napkins. For a novel effect, blue glass vases have been put to use as candle holders.

On the table opposite, wicker cheese trays are used as place mats over individual dishtowel runners. The napkins—which have been loosely knotted, rather than folded, to maintain a casual mood—and the runners were chosen to coordinate with the blue of the chair cushions. An ironstone pitcher serves as an informal wine decanter, and a bowl of lemons—rather than the more customary fruit basket—provides not only color, but also the fresh scent of citrus.

Casual yet elegant, the table setting opposite mixes natural materials and plain pottery with crystal wine glasses and traditional, shell-patterned flatware.

Focus on Color

Bright teapots, pitchers, and dinnerware create an eye-catching setting on the marble-topped table at right. Newly made by the Hall China Company, the pieces are reproductions of the highly collectible wares the company produced from the 1920s to the 1950s. Checkerboard bandannas placed informally on the plates enhance the light-hearted mood.

B y using color, you can readily create an original look for your table. At left, marble tiles set off a mix of large dinner plates and pear-shaped platters that reflects the bright color scheme of the hand-painted chairs. But here dinnerware is only part of the table design: the vivid fruits and flowers are also a studied match.

To create the fanciful table for tea, above, an arrangement of colorful polka-dot, solid, and checked dishes was composed on a tablecloth stenciled with a floral pattern. Cups, platters, bowls, and plates like these were made in a broad range of colors from the 1930s to the 1960s and are still widely available today. You can collect pieces in the shades you like, then mix them together for a different setting daily.

The tea setting above features an assortment of colorful 20th-century pottery. The squared-off plates are Riviera ware, which was made between 1938 and 1950, and the cups and saucers are reproductions of Harlequin pottery, sold exclusively by the F.W. Woolworth Company until the 1950s.

A Country Tea

Hosting a country tea is one of the simplest, yet most elegant, ways to entertain. And even when the fare is as humble as orange pekoe, muffins, and jam, you can create an attractive setting like the one above just by using a linen table runner, pretty china, and a basket or two for serving food.

The most important element of any tea party is the pot. Like tea itself, which was first imported to Europe from China during the 17th century, the teapot owes its origins to the Orient. The designs of the first European teapots were influenced by Chinese water or wine jugs in which the Orientals prepared their brew. Early British teapots were elongated, resembling many of the coffeepots we know today. Although it is unclear why the pot didn't stay tall, a shorter pot eventually evolved, taking on round, pear-shaped, polygonal, oval, and rectangular forms. Those with flat bottoms often came with stands to protect the table; others had feet or rimmed bases.

While formal teas once called for matched sets, today's casual lifestyle permits you to mix teapots, cups, and plates. The pots opposite are just a few of the many types, both antique and contemporary, that you might want to collect. See page 169 for more information.

Reproduction "Pagoda" teapot

English terra-cotta pot, c. 1850

English Royal Minton

English Ridgway porcelain, c. 1815

Reproduction majolica "bird's nest"

American graniteware, c. 1860

Contemporary Italian earthenware

American sterling silver, c. 1900

Reproduction "Blue Canton"

Contemporary hand-painted ceramic

Contemporary blue spongeware

Rare English agateware, c. 1800

Fragrant bulb flowers are interspersed with small and large candles to make an informal setting for the table above. The soft color scheme of gray, pink, and white heralds spring.

Even if winter's chill still lingers, you can bring warmth to your home by setting a table that hints of spring. A combination of pretty linens, delicate china, and the fragrance of fresh blooms will summon expectations of the sunny months ahead.

To create the informal—and sweet-smelling—setting above, hyacinths, crocuses, and an amaryllis were placed randomly across a simple wooden table. Bulb flowers like these, which can be forced early in individual pots, make an equally effective centerpiece when clustered in a tight group; or you can set a pot at each place. Here, pale gray dinner plates, floral-patterned napkins, woven place mats, and an imaginative mix of candles complete the inviting table decor.

Narcissus and freesia add spring cheer to the windowside table opposite, where a comfortable wing chair has been pulled close to the small table for a quiet meal alone. The blue-and-white patterns of Delft chinaware—a dinner plate, flower bricks, and a wine carafe—create a refreshing color scheme with the yellow and white flowers.

The earthenware pieces, part of a larger collection, were the inspiration for the design of the tabletop, which is decorated with a trompe l'oeil painting of Delft tiles. A brass candlestick and a starched linen napkin add elegance to this charming scene.

Spring Settings

Antique Delftware and clusters of fresh flowers, left, transform a side table into a cozy setting for dining. The cheerful colors help brighten a gray day.

Secondhand Finds

D ishes and serving pieces don't have to match—or be expensive—to make an effective table design. Clever place settings can be gathered, piece by piece, from flea markets, garage sales, secondhand stores, and antique shops. Even your attic may prove a source of unusual tableware and accessories.

The red-checked tablecloth appliquéd with polka-dot pottery on the breakfast table opposite, for example, was discovered in perfect condition at a rummage sale. Its informal country look is enhanced by inexpensive bandanna napkins and novelty shakers in the shape of chicks.

Equally eclectic, the place setting above is made up almost entirely of unmatched items. Here a variety of Depression-glass pieces, including stemware and salt cellars, are combined, while flatware with plastic handles is teamed with an enamel spoon. Tumblers and egg cups serve as impromptu flower vases.

Flea markets and thrift shops are ideal sources for tableware such as the pieces above. The "compartment plate" is typical of the dishes used in homes, restaurants, and cafeterias from the 1930s to the 1950s.

Plain dinnerware, opposite, complements a bright mix of linens, flatware, and glasses; white shows off food and garnishes to advantage. The checked tablecloth dates from around 1935.

COUNTRY SHAKERS

When you reach for the salt and pepper shakers at your next country meal, why not let them be a plump tomato couple, a set of ripe watermelons, or a "pepper pie" and a "salt à la mode?"

First patented around the turn of the century, novelty shakers were usually made of ceramic, plastic, or glass. They were—and still are—often created as souvenirs for tourist attractions and state fairs or as gift catalogue items, and were also made as promotion pieces for products like Planters peanuts and Acme beer. Novelty shakers were particularly popular in the 1940s and 1950s, when "salt and pepper clubs" for collectors proliferated.

Shakers like those shown here—made in Japan, Europe, and the United States—are usually reasonably priced: mint-condition sets, still in their boxes, are the most valuable. Before buying, be sure to check that it is indeed a *pair* of shakers that you are considering. The salt shaker always has more holes or larger holes than the pepper; so if the holes are identical you may be purchasing two salts or two peppers. If you are collecting seriously, do not remove the manufacturer's or import company's tags, which can enhance the value of the shakers.

This roundup of country shakers includes just a few of the thousands of types still available at reasonable prices.

Summer
Settings

White linens, a bouquet of white flowers, and a willow-bark basket filled with fresh peaches create a cool look for the small table above.

Whether you choose to dine outside or to bring the outdoors in with fresh flowers and crisp fabrics, refreshing whites and soft pastels are ideal colors for summer tables.

The inviting setting above uses the simplest, yet most complex, of color schemes: white on white. An 1880s half-round table (bearing its original paint) has been draped with a starched linen cloth and set with white pottery, including an antique creamware plate, sugar bowl, and creamer. A bouquet of flowers and a basket of ripe peaches enhance the summertime mood.

Sea and sky make a striking backdrop for the gardenside deck opposite, where white Lloyd loom wicker chairs surround a weathered table that is set for a midafternoon tea. Pale floral-patterned dishes pick up the pinks of the roses in the nearby flower garden and anchor the linen napkins against sea breezes.

On the table opposite, linens and china in a combination of pastel colors and white create a carefree summertime mood. Apples and bramble roses, casually arranged in a woven ceramic basket, make a beautiful, color-coordinated centerpiece.

A blend of old and new adds to the charm of the elegant table setting at right. Dainty Victorian-era wine glasses are paired with contemporary water goblets of engraved glass. And new lace-bordered napkins are coordinated with an heirloom tablecloth.

Country Elegance

Embroidered linens and delicate porcelain contribute to the sophisticated look of these two country tabletops. Despite their elegance, the settings are not staid. Nontraditional touches, such as unmatched tablewares and imaginative—even casual—centerpieces, give these tables an easy grace.

On the table at left, brass and silver candlesticks are especially eye-catching because of their unconventional arrangement. Instead of being placed symmetrically, the candlesticks have been grouped to form two off-center "centerpieces." Their different styles and heights add further visual interest.

Here an antique cutwork linen tablecloth has been used to set off the English china, a reproduction of a 19th-century floral pattern. Double-handled soup cups with underplates, crystal stemware, monogrammed silverware, and individual salt shakers also add elegance.

A tureen of apples brings a touch of country earthiness to the otherwise formal setting above. The handmade lace cloth adds soft texture to the table while letting the wood show through. English blue-and-white china from the late 1800s was chosen in different, but complementary, patterns for variety. The notion of "anything goes" also works in the odd pairing of an embossed silver spoon with 1940s flatware fitted with imitation ivory handles.

A handmade linen tablecloth from the 1920s or 1930s brings a look of grace to the elegant country table
above, set with 19th-century English china.

CREATING A CENTERPIECE

While filling a vase with fresh flowers is one of the easiest ways to dress up a country table, a memorable centerpiece doesn't have to include flowers at all. The season, a party theme, or even everyday items you have on hand can also inspire ideas for table decorations. Be inventive, but don't get so carried away that your decoration blocks conversation.

Take a cue from the photographs here, which show how the same table looks with four different centerpieces, or consider the following ideas. If you're having neighbors over for ice cream on a hot summer day, make a colorful centerpiece with an arrangement of old-fashioned sundae glasses filled with colored sugars and chocolate sprinkles. For a birthday celebration, tie ribbons around the flatware, scatter confetti over the table, and wrap party favors as the centerpiece.

Favorite mementos and collectibles can be put to use as festive table decorations. Move framed family pictures onto the table for an anniversary party. Or, create an autum-

A chocolate lover's dessert party, above, is even more tempting when old pewter chocolate molds and a basket of sweets are the centerpiece. For a brunch or an omelet party, right, let a wire egg holder set your theme. Use egg cups as salt cellars or jam pots and add ceramic chickens to complete the rustic country feeling.

158

nal centerpiece by letting a few duck decoys "nest" in baskets of straw.

Your grocery store or farmers' market can also provide the makings for inventive centerpieces. Take advantage of seasonal produce to create a lush still life. Lemons or strawberries piled in bright sponge-ware bowls will draw guests to a summertime buffet. In the winter, red and green apples placed in a burl bowl are equally effective. During the Christmas season, popcorn and cranberries in beribboned baskets—along with pine cones and boughs—make a good centerpiece, and you can also ask guests to help you string them into garlands after the meal is over.

And don't feel you must always use traditional candlesticks. Experiment with putting candles in pieces of gnarled driftwood· or in cored apples. Or look around your pantry for additional inspiration. Heart-shaped pastry tins can hold candles for a Valentine's Day party; a four-sided grater serves as a pierced-tin lantern; and a muffin tin will hold a dozen votive candles.

Create a fantasy centerpiece for children—or simply the young at heart—above, by filling vintage syrup jars with candy and letting wooden animals graze in a "field" of lollipops. At left, a basket filled with sweet and hot peppers becomes a colorful centerpiece for a Mexican dinner. Twine balls serve as unexpected candle holders.

Cane-back chairs pulled up to a Louis XVI country writing table create the setting for an intimate autumn supper, above.

Autumn leaves and late harvest vegetables, nuts, and crisp apples are only a small part of a generous fall bounty that lends itself naturally to creative table decorating. To strike a country mood, you can simply arrange a few acorns, chestnuts, and tiny pumpkins by each place setting, or fill a basket or antique colander with ears of Indian corn. For a more elegant feeling, consider arranging sprays of dried wheat or rye in a vase or pitcher, then tucking a stem or two into a folded napkin at each guest's place.

On the table above, an earthenware casserole has been filled with gourds to create an autumnal setting for a candlelit supper. The simple straw place mats, bamboo-handled flatware, and yellow-checked napkins are perfectly suited to a relaxing fall meal.

On the dinner table opposite, a wooden bowl brimming with dried leaves is an easy but effective centerpiece. This handsome tabletop derives even more fall feeling from the warm glow of candlelight and from the tablecloth and napkins made of contrasting mini-print fabrics in rustic colors. Linens like these can readily be sewn at home from fabric remnants.

Autumn Settings

The warm, robust colors of fall are an integral part of the seasonal table decorations at left. The centerpiece makes use of autumn foliage.

Dining Alternatives

Not all meals call for sitting down at the kitchen or dining room table. When a crowd is expected, presenting a buffet is often the best way to feed your guests. And if you are eating alone, you may simply want to pull a tray table up to a comfortable chair and settle down with a good book. An attractive setting will make either occasion enjoyable.

Arranged for a country buffet, the dining room at left is ready to welcome guests to an afternoon wine and cheese party. To keep traffic flowing, the stemware, cutlery, and napkins have been placed on the pine huntboard next to plates stacked in a wooden plate rack. On the long dining table, a shallow woven basket holds an appetizing arrangement of fruits and cheeses, while a rustic twig basket is used to serve loaves of bread. Two mid-1900s birdhouses and an old newel post make novel table decorations.

Favorite collectibles and mementos can also add charm—or a feeling of nostalgia—to a personal place setting. The hand-painted English tray table above, for example, was set with a framed watercolor, a pitcher of roses, and English carpet bowls—once used in a popular 19th-century parlor game. A rose-print linen napkin and a majolica plate were chosen for their color and complementary floral theme.

Whether you are serving many guests at a buffet or dining alone, a thoughtful presentation will make the meal more enjoyable. Fresh spring flowers and rustic baskets are used creatively on the buffet, left, while a few accessories enhance the look of the tray for one, above.

QUILT SQUARE NAPKINS

To make quilt square napkins, purchase vintage quilt squares at antique shows or from quilt dealers. Quilt squares are fabric pieces that may have been made for a quilt but never used, or sections that were cut from damaged quilts. They come in many sizes, but are often about 6½ inches square. To make dinner napkins like those here, first stitch together four small quilt squares, or use one large square. If desired, separate the squares with colorful borders.

A. Lace should be basted to right side of quilt square, with binding seam aligned along fabric edge.

MATERIALS

· One 12- to 20-inch quilt square for napkin front ·
· One 12- to 20-inch fabric square for napkin back ·
· Approximately 2½ yards ruffled lace edging of width desired ·
· Dressmaker pins · Thread ·

DIRECTIONS

1. Carefully iron the quilt square and place it right side up. To start the lace edging, place the bound edge of the lace along one edge of the square so that the ruffles face the center of the square. Leave about a 5-inch "tail" of lace extending beyond the starting corner.

2. Pin the lace to the fabric, inserting the pins at a right angle to the edge of the square. Pin through the binding seam of the lace, then into the fabric, ¼ inch from the edge. Pin across the first edge of the square, stopping ¼ inch from the corner.

3. Turn the bound edge of the lace around the corner, clipping ¼ inch into the lace binding to ease if necessary. As you turn the corner, fold the lace into a tuck, and pin. Continue to pin the lace around two more edges and two more corners, leaving the fourth edge free. Baste the lace to the square along the binding seam (Illustration A).

4. Pin the lace to the fourth edge, stopping about 5 inches from the corner. Pick up the tail of lace, turn the bound edge around the corner as above, and pin. Cut off any extra lace and sew the raw lace ends together by hand. Baste the lace to this edge as above.

5. Stitch the lace to the square along the basting, being careful not to catch the extra lace tucked at the corners in the seams. Remove the pins. With right sides together and edges even, place the quilt square over the fabric for the napkin back and pin together, with pins at right angles to the edges. Stitch a ¼-inch seam all the way around the square (Illustration B), leaving 5 inches open on the last edge.

6. To finish the napkin, remove the pins and basting, clip corners, and iron the seams open. Pull the napkin through the opening to turn it right side out. From the inside, gently push out the corner seams with a wooden knitting needle or another blunt-pointed instrument to make them open up fully into square corners. At the open edge, turn under the ¼-inch seam allowance and pin the front and back together. Using small hand stitches, close the opening (Illustration C). Remove the pins and iron the napkin.

B. Napkin front and back are stitched together over pins. Pins and basting are removed before napkin is inverted.

C. After napkin is turned right side out, opening should be sewn closed with small hand stitches just below lace.

Winter Settings

Rich colors and appetizing foods distinguish these two fireside settings. For an indoor wintertime picnic in the cabin dining room, left, a homespun cloth was spread out and set with spatterware plates and stoneware mugs. Equipped with a variety of iron utensils, the hearth can be used for preparing soups and stews, popping corn, roasting chestnuts, and warming bread or plum pudding. Here cider is mulled in a graniteware kettle not far from the fire.

The deep red color scheme above enhances a setting for an afternoon tea. A 19th-century paisley shawl covers the fireside table, set with simple hand-painted cups and saucers. A cluster of grapes and a few Red Bartlett pears form the casual, edible centerpiece.

Firelight, and candles set in mid-19th-century molds made of pewter and wood, cast a warm light on the indoor picnic at left.

A Victorian paisley shawl decorated with the traditional swirl pattern makes an imaginative tablecloth for the winter tea setting above.

Selected Reading

Barber, Edwin Atlee, Luke Vincent Lockwood, and Hollis French. *The Ceramic, Furniture, and Silver Collectors' Glossary*. New York: Da Capo Press, 1976.

Barnard, Julian. *Victorian Ceramic Tiles*. New York: Mayflower Books, 1979.

Belden, Louise Conway. *The Festive Tradition: Table Decoration and Desserts in America, 1650-1900*. New York: W. W. Norton & Company, 1983.

Bosker, Gideon. *Great Shakes: Salt and Pepper for All Tastes*. New York: Abbeville Press, 1986.

Boyce, Charles. *Dictionary of Furniture*. New York: Roundtable Press, 1985.

Carlo, Joyce W. *Trammels, Trenchers, and Tartlets*. Old Saybrook, Conn.: Peregrine Press, 1982.

Celehar, Jane H. *Kitchens and Gadgets 1920 to 1950*. Lombard, Ill.: Wallace-Homestead, 1982.

Coffin, Margaret. *The History and Folklore of American Country Tinware 1700-1900*. New York: Galahad Books, 1968.

Cooper, Jane. *Woodstove Cookery: At Home on the Range*. Pownal, Vt.: Storey Communications, 1977.

Feild, Rachael. *Irons in the Fire: A History of Cooking Equipment*. Wiltshire, England: Crowood Press, 1984.

Fennimore, Donald L. *Silver and Pewter*. New York: Alfred A. Knopf, 1984.

Franklin, Linda Campbell. *300 Years of Kitchen Collectibles*. Florence, Ala.: Books Americana, 1984.

Franklin, Linda Campbell. *From Hearth to Cookstove*. Florence, Ala.: House of Collectibles, 1976.

Gold, Charles, and Peri Wolfman. *The Perfect Setting*. New York: Harry N. Abrams, 1985.

Gould, Mary Earle. *Early American Wooden Ware and Other Kitchen Utensils*. Rutland, Vt.: Charles E. Tuttle Company, 1962.

Grover, Kathryn, ed. *Dining in America 1850-1900*. Amherst: University of Massachusetts Press, 1987.

Kauffman, Henry J. *American Copper and Brass*. Camden, N.J.: Thomas Nelson & Sons, 1968.

Ketchum, William C., Jr. *Pottery and Porcelain*. New York: Alfred A. Knopf, 1983.

Ketchum, William C., Jr. *American Country Pottery: Yellowware and Spongeware*. New York: Alfred A. Knopf, 1987.

Lantz, Louise K. *Old American Kitchenware: 1725-1925*. Hanover, Pa.: Everybodys Press, 1970.

Marshall, Jo. *Kitchenware*. Radnor, Pa: Chilton Book Company, 1976.

McCulloch, Lou W. *Paper Americana: A Collector's Guide*. San Diego: A.S. Barnes and Company, 1980.

Montgomery, Charles F. *A History of American Pewter*. New York: Praeger Publishers, 1973.

Niles, Bo. *Country Kitchens*. New York: Roundtable Press, 1985.

Phipps, Frances. *Colonial Kitchens, Their Furnishings, and Their Gardens*. New York: Hawthorn Books, 1972.

Pinto, Edward H. *Treen and Other Wooden Bygones: An Encyclopedia and Social History*. London: Bell & Hyman, 1969.

Riley, Noël. *Tile Art: A History of Decorative Ceramic Tiles*. Secaucus, N.J.: Chartwell Books, 1987.

Schiffer, Herbert, Peter Schiffer, and Nancy Schiffer. *Antique Iron: Survey of American and English Forms, Fifteenth through Nineteenth Centuries*. Exton, Pa.: Schiffer Publishing, 1979.

Smith, Michael. *The Afternoon Tea Book*. New York: Atheneum, 1986.

Spargo, John. *Early American Pottery and China*. Rutland, Vt.: Charles E. Tuttle Company, 1974.

Time-Life Books. *Kitchens*. Alexandria, Va.: Time-Life Books, 1985.

Warren, Geoffrey. *Kitchen Bygones: A Collector's Guide*. London: Souvenir Press, 1984.

Webster, Donald Blake. *Decorated Stoneware Pottery of North America*. Rutland, Vt.: Charles E. Tuttle Company, 1971.

Photography Credits

Cover, frontispiece, and pages 10-13 (except 11 right), 18-19, 21, 28-31, 34-37 (except 37 right), 46-48, 54, 59, 64-65, 77 (except bottom), 81 (right), 85-88, 99-100, 108-112, 118 (left), 119, 131, 134, 136, 145, 149, 155, 156, 160, 161, 167: George Ross. Pages 8, 22-23, 61, 76, 101, 113, 116, 138, 150, 163: Jon Elliott. Pages 11 (right), 20, 24 (left), 26-27, 37 (right), 44-45, 50, 52, 56-57, 62-63, 70 (right), 71 (left), 78-79, 84 (right), 89, 92-95, 98, 102-103, 106-107, 114-115, 122-123, 128-129, 137, 140-141, 146, 152-154, 157, 164-166: Steven Mays. Pages 14, 16 (left), 82-83, 147 (except second row, right): Simeone Ricci. Pages 15, 96-97, 147 (second row, right): David Phelps. Pages 16-17 (except 16 left), 60: Ralph Bogertman. Pages 24-25 (except 24 left): David Glomb/*Home* Magazine; 144: David Glomb. Pages 32-33: Sketches by George Bell, inked by Walter Hilmers Jr./H. L. Commercial Art. Pages 38-39, left to right: Kit Barry; Kit Barry; Kitchen Arts and Letters; Culver Pictures; Kit Barry; Kitchen Arts and Letters; The Glusker Group; Kit Barry; Culver Pictures. Pages 40-42: William P. Steele. Pages 51, 58, 91, 127: Michael Skott. Page 53: Smallbone. Pages 55, 77 (bottom), 80, 143: Bradley Olman. Pages 66-67, 125: Laurie Black/ARX. Pages 68-69, 75, 104: Laurie Black and Roz Bannish, ARX/*Home* Magazine. Pages 70 (left), 71 (right): Blue Ridge Institute. Pages 72-73, 126, 133, 139, 142, 148: Chris Mead. Page 74: Fred George. Page 81 (left): Jessie Walker. Page 84 (left): Karen Bussolini. Pages 90, 118 (right): J. Barry O'Rourke/The Stock Market. Page 105: Steven Mark Needham. Pages 120-121: Blair Seitz. Pages 124, 151: Lilo Raymond/©1987 Meredith Corporation. All Rights Reserved. Reprinted from *Ladies' Home Journal* Magazine. Page 130: Daniel Eifert. Page 132: Robert Perron. Pages 158-159: Ron Brello, Jr. Page 162: Bill Waldron. Page 171: Schematic drawing by Tim Jeffs.

Prop Credits

The Editors would like to thank the following for their courtesy in lending items for photography. Items not listed below are privately owned. **Page 8**: banister-back chairs—June Worrell Antiques, Houston, TX. **Page 11**: wire basket—Bonnie and Floyd Wombles, Summer Hill, IL. **Page 14**: antique brass pepper shaker, caster, trivet, lidded saucepan, and grater—James II Galleries, Ltd., NYC; copper saucepan and utensils—Charles Lamalle, NYC. **Page 15**: collection of antique copper and brass—Pat Guthman Antiques, Southport, CT. **Page 16**: Nantucket lightship basket—Four Winds Craft Guild, Inc., Nantucket, MA. **Pages 16-17**: designed by Trudy Dujardin Interiors, Westport, CT. **Page 18**: scherenschnitte—Claudia and Perry Hopf, Kennebunk, ME; grain-painted frames—Carroll Hopf, Kennebunk, ME. **Pages 20-21**: dried-apple wreath made by Judy Brauner/The Cinnamon Stick, Hummelstown, PA. **Pages 22-23**: window treatment and tablecloth fabric—Waverly Fabrics, NYC; window treatment and tablecloth made by Barbara Valentine's Grandma's Curtains, Chester, NJ. **Pages 24-25**: designed by Van-Martin Rowe Architectural and Interior Design, Los Angeles, CA. **Pages 26-27**: stools painted by Frank Lavin, Jr./Disenos, Inc., Jackson Heights, NY; precut stencils used on stool—Gail Grisi Stenciling, Inc., Haddonfield, NJ. **Pages 28-29**: designed by Richard Lowell Neas, NYC; "pantry," range hood, and refrigerator doors painted by Richard Lowell Neas. **Pages 50-51**: pierced-steel cabinets—Bill Conn, Charlottesville, VA; stenciling—Nancy Conn, Charlottesville, VA. **Page 52**: precut stencils used for cabinet—Gail Grisi Stenciling, Inc., Haddonfield, NJ. **Page 54**: designed by Ronald Bricke of Ronald Bricke & Associates, NYC. **Pages 56-57**: Background wallcovering: "Yonville," from *Victoria Morland's Farmhouse in Provence*—Raintree Designs. Top shelf: all items—Hall China Co., East Liverpool, OH. Middle shelf: small ramekins and teapot—Hall China Co.; glassware—Libbey Glass, Toledo, OH; all other items—Apilco/Elite Limoges, NYC; wallcovering border, "Grandes Indiennes," from *Victoria Morland's Farmhouse in Provence*—Raintree Designs, NYC. Bottom shelf: mugs—Hall China Co.; glassware—Libbey Glass; all other items—Apilco/Elite Limoges; lace valance, "Cottage Garden"—Linen and Lace, Washington, MO. **Page 59**: designed by Richard Lowell Neas, NYC. **Page 62**: Top photo: mail baskets—Basketville, Inc., Putney, VT; spice chest—The Strawberry Tree, Newburyport, MA; cotton dishtowels—Trade Associates Group, Chicago, IL. Bottom photo: mugs—Waechtersbach USA, Inc., Kansas City, MO; porcelain spoons, pitchers, creamers—Apilco/Elite Limoges, NYC. **Page 63**: Top photo: selected items—Pantry & Hearth/Gail Lettick Collection, NYC. Bottom photo: copper cookware—Charles Lamalle, NYC; Calphalon, anodized aluminum cookware—Comerical Aluminum Cookware Co., Toledo, OH. **Pages 64-65**: designed by Madeline Armeson, Dennisport, MA. **Pages 66-67**: designed by Michaele Thunen, Berkeley, CA; cabinets—Flying A Cabinets, Petaluma, CA; space planner—Stuart McIntee of Charles Lester & Associates, San Francisco, CA. **Pages 70-71**, left to right: Blue Ridge Institute, Ferrum College, Ferrum, VA; Cynthia Beneduce

Antiques, NYC; Cynthia Beneduce Antiques; Blue Ridge Institute. **Pages 78-79**: see tile schematic, page 171: (1) made by Flint Michigan Tile Co., MI, c. 1920—Malvina I. Solomon, Inc., NYC; (2) made by Trent Tile Co., NJ, c. 1900—Malvina I. Solomon, Inc.; (3) made by Trent Tile Co.—Gem Antiques, NYC; (4) made by The Providential Tile Works, NJ—Gem Antiques; (5) made by American Encaustic Tile Co., OH, c. 1910—Malvina I. Solomon, Inc.; (6) made by J. and J. G. Low, MA, c. 1883—Malvina I. Solomon, Inc.; (7) made by Grueby, MA, c. 1915—Malvina I. Solomon, Inc.; (8) made by Mercer Tile, PA—Gem Antiques; (9) "Radish," Spanish—Country Floors, NYC; (10) "Culinarios," Portuguese—Country Floors; (11) made by International Tile Co., NY, c. 1900—Malvina I. Solomon, Inc.; (12) fruit border, Spanish—Country Floors; (13) Victorian transfer tile, hand-decorated, adaptation—Designs in Tile, Foster City, CA; (14) "Rosier" border, French—Country Floors; (15) Heritage Series, #HT-6—Summitville Tiles, Inc., Summitville, OH; (16) "Olambrillos" star, Spanish—Country Floors; (17) folk tile series, hand-painted, adaptation—Designs in Tile; (18) William De-Morgan historic reproduction, hand-painted—Designs in Tile; (19, 20) "Royal Makkum," Dutch—Country Floors; (21) Herbs & Spice, #HS-4—Summitville Tiles, Inc.; (22) hand-painted, original design—Marion Grebow, NYC; (23) "Olambrillos" relief, Spanish—Country Floors; (24) hand-painted and original designs—Rabbit Artworks, Santa Fe, NM; (25, 26) hand-crafted and painted—Terra Designs, Dover, NJ; (27) "Triangoli," Italian—Country Floors; (28) hand-painted and original designs—Rabbit Artworks; (29) "Ma Primrose," Spanish—Country Floors. **Page 80**: designed by Motif Designs, New Rochelle, NY. **Page 82**: vinyl flooring, clockwise from top left: "Bristol," real red/black, #40175—Congoleum Corp.; "Monaco," quicksilver/burgundy, #62023—Congoleum; "Floral Key," mauve blossom,

#71043—Tarkett, Inc.; "Cameo," ebony, #86158—Congoleum; "Palen Tile," light regatta, #40154—Congoleum; "Orchard Park," sienna hickory, #75177—Tarkett; "Parkway," black/white, #50077—Congoleum; "Barrett Brick," terra-cotta, #65832—Armstrong World Industries, Inc.; "Avondale," blue, #87622—Armstrong; "Rondelle," regatta/white, #17052—Congoleum; "Linden Court," slate gray, #61038—Tarkett; "Autumn Blossom," multicolor, #66021—Armstrong; "Kennett Square," concord white, #54633—Tarkett; "Harland Court," red clay, #82019—Armstrong. **Page 83**: vinyl flooring, clockwise from top left: "Fulton Square," malibu sand, #86149—Congoleum; "Holly Hill," black/white, #10001—Congoleum; "Somerset," colonial red, #37020—Congoleum; "Autumn Blossom," gray/burgundy, #66025—Armstrong; "Cameo," light regatta blue, #86154—Congoleum; "Linden Court," paver red, #61037—Tarkett; "New Mark," multicolor, #69580—Armstrong; "Fontenay," dusty graphite, #62075—Congoleum; "Corbett," blue, #61272—Armstrong; "Robin Court," colebrooke brown, #71057—Tarkett; "Liberty Square," black/white, #33017—Congoleum; "Pauley Place," medium blue, #47140—Tarkett; "Stonegate," slate gray, #37001 —Congoleum; "Chadsford," mint green, #87685 —Armstrong. **Page 84**, right: stenciling by Nancy Conn, Charlottesville, VA. **Page 89**: kitchenware—Katie Johnson Antiques, Westlake, LA. **Pages 92-93**: bakeware and accessories—Meryle Evans, NYC, and Pantry & Hearth/Gail Lettick Collection, NYC. **Pages 94-95**: iron and steel collection and other kitchen accessories—Sandy Worrell (June Worrell Antiques), Houston, TX. **Pages 96-97**: hearth cooking utensils—Pat Guthman Antiques, Southport, CT. **Pages 102-103**: spongeware collection—Patricia Smith. **Page 105**: wallcovering, "All in Clover," from *Victoria Morland's Book of English Country Decoration*—Raintree Designs, NYC; Depression glass—Jeff's Uniques, Feasterville, PA. **Pages**

106-107: toaster collection—Howard Hazelcorn, Teaneck, NJ. **Pages 114-115**: cookbooks and pamphlets—collection of Bonnie Slotnick, NYC. **Page 125**: designed by Michaele Thunen, Berkeley, CA. **Pages 128-129**: wallcovering, "Antoinette," from *Victoria Morland's Farmhouse in Provence*—Raintree Designs, NYC; fabrics—The Watermelon Patch, Manhasset, NY. **Page 130**: designed by Antine Associates, Fort Lee, NJ; wallcovering—Foremost Wallcoverings, Ontario, CAN. **Page 131**: designed by Madeline Armeson, Dennisport, MA. **Pages 136-137**: kitchen table accessories—Katie Johnson Antiques, Westlake, LA. **Page 138**: window treatment and tablecloth fabric—Waverly Fabrics, NYC; window treatment and tablecloth made by Barbara Valentine's Grandma's Curtains, Chester, NJ. **Pages 140-141**: Top row, left to right: pewter spoons—privately owned; horn flatware—Richard Lowell Neas, NYC; beaded flatware—privately owned; stag flatware—Richard Lowell Neas; wood and pewter flatware—Vito Giallo Antiques, NYC; bone and steel flatware—Lost & Found Antiques, Kensington, MD; ebony and pewter flatware, coin silver spoon—Clifton Anderson Antiques of Lexington, KY. Bottom row, left to right: agate flatware, Tiffany sterling silver flatware, mother of pearl fruit fork and knife—Vito Giallo Antiques; Bakelite flatware—Mood Indigo, NYC; "Shell," sterling silver flatware, Williamsburg reproduction—Kirk Stieff, Baltimore, MD; "Buttercup," sterling silver flatware—Gorham, Providence, RI; "Oak Leaf" handwrought sterling silver flatware—Old Newbury Crafters, Amesbury, MA; "Red Octagon" ceramic flatware—Thaxton & Co., NYC. **Page 144**: room designed by Van-Martin Rowe Architectural and Interior Design, Los Angeles, CA; dinnerware, pitchers, and teapots—Hall China Co., East Liverpool, OH; chairs painted by Jane Anderson, Los Angeles, CA; highchair painted by Gary R. Sipe of Van-Martin Rowe Architectural and Interior Design. **Page 146**: "Mariposa" china—Villeroy &

Boch, NYC; coin design baby pillow sham used as tray liner—Vito Giallo Antiques, NYC; wallcovering, "Clover Plaid," from *Victoria Morland's Book of English Country Decoration*—Raintree Designs, NYC. **Page 147**: Top row, left to right: "Pagoda" teapot—Mottahedeh & Co., NYC; painted terra-cotta teapot—Vito Giallo Antiques, NYC; English Royal Minton teapot—privately owned. Second row, left to right: teapot with stand—Bardith Ltd., NYC; ceramic teapot with bird—The Haldon Group, Irving, TX; graniteware teapot—Pat Guthman Antiques, Southport, CT. Third row, left to right: earthenware teapot—Gear, NYC; sterling silver teapot—Vito Giallo Antiques; "Blue Canton" teapot—Mottahedeh & Co. Bottom row, left to right: ceramic floral teapot—The Haldon Group; blue spongeware teapot—Bennington Potters, Bennington, VT; agateware teapot—Vito Giallo Antiques. **Page 149**: painted floor, baseboard, window frame, and table "tiles" designed and painted by Richard Lowell Neas, NYC. **Pages 152-153**: salt and pepper shakers—Barbara London, NYC, and Laura Auerbach

Bernstein, Great Neck, NY. **Page 154**: painted table—Cinda Wombles-Pettigrew, White Bear Lake, MN; linen curtains—International Linen Association, NYC; creamware pitcher used as vase, twig napkin ring—Wolfman Gold & Good Co., NYC. **Page 156**: room designed by Madeline Armeson, Dennisport, MA. **Page 158**: Top photo: wallcovering, "Summer Oak," from *Victoria Morland's Book of English Country Decoration*—Raintree Designs, NYC; antique pewter chocolate molds—Funchie, Bunkers, Gaks and Gleeks, NYC, and Laura Fisher/Antique Quilts & Americana, NYC; lace runner—Rue de France, Newport, RI. Bottom photo: ceramic hens and chicks—Funchie, Bunkers, Gaks and Gleeks; quilt square napkin—C. J. Brown/American Antiques, Textiles & Accessories, Staten Island, NY. **Page 159**: Top photo: wooden animals, glass animal jars—Funchie, Bunkers, Gaks and Gleeks, NYC; cotton dishtowel—Trade Associate Group, Chicago, IL. **Page 160**: room designed by Richard Lowell Neas, NYC. **Page 162**: room designed by Motif Designs, New Rochelle, NY; wallcovering, "Isadora"—

Ralph Lauren, NYC; baskets—Be Seated, NYC; wicker bottle and plate rack—Cobweb Antiques, NYC; glassware and green pottery bowls—Pottery Barn, NYC; napkins, bobbin candlesticks, dinner plates—Gear, NYC. **Page 163**: hand-painted English tray table, majolica plate, carpet bowls, printed lace napkin, bowl and pitcher, and framed watercolor—Private Collections, Cedarhurst, NY. **Pages 164-165**: Kenmore sewing machine—Sears Roebuck & Co.; quilt squares—C. J. Brown, American Antiques, Textiles & Accessories, Staten Island, NY; dinnerware, candlesticks, salt and pepper shakers, and water pitcher—Quimper Faience, Stonington, CT; hand-blown glasses—Simon Pearce, NYC; antique pine table—Evergreen Antiques, NYC; fabric used for quilt square backs—Watermelon Patch, Manhasset, NY; wallcovering, "Trelawny," from *Victoria Morland's Book of English Country Decoration*—Raintree Designs, NYC. **Page 167**: Victorian paisley shawl—Laura Fisher/Antique Quilts & Americana, NYC.

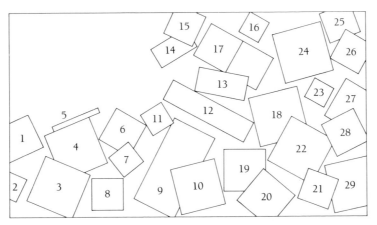

Schematic for tiles appearing on pages 78 and 79.

Index

Acknowledgments

Our thanks to Jane Anderson, Madeline Armeson, Judy and Alex Awrylo, Ronald Bricke, Bette and David Chenault, Nancy and Bill Conn, Rika and Daniel Cornwell, Jimmy Cramer, Barbara and Player Crosby, Diane and Chip Durell, Vito Giallo, Margaret and Charles Gure, Pat Guthman, Ed Haverty, Claudia and Carroll Hopf, Katie and Bobby Johnson, Barbara Lipps, Mary Ann Miles, Howard Monroe, J. Roderick Moore, Richard Lowell Neas, Gail Peachin, Lyn Peterson, Barbara and Charles Randau, Barbara and Julie Radcliffe Rogers, Van-Martin Rowe, Dona and Fred Schuller, Mitch Sreidlin, Elinor E. Stearns, Joy and Bill Thomas, Don Thornton, Michaele Thunen, Barbara Valentine, Dot and Bud Walters, Kathy and Ken Wilson, Sandy Worrell, and Phyllis Wrynn.

Second printing
Published simultaneously in Canada
School and library distribution by Silver Burdett Company,
Morristown, New Jersey

TIME-LIFE is a trademark of Time Incorporated U.S.A.

Production by Giga Communications, Inc.
Printed in U.S.A.

Library of Congress Cataloging-in-Publication Data

The Country kitchen.
p. cm. — (American country)
Includes index.
ISBN 0-8094-6754-2. ISBN 0-8094-6755-0 (lib. bdg.)
1. Kitchens. 2. Interior decoration—United States.
3. Decoration and ornament, Rustic—United States.
I. Time-Life Books. II. Series
NK2117.K5C67 1988
747.7'97—dc 19   88-16078
CIP

American Country was created by Rebus, Inc., and published by Time-Life Books.

REBUS, INC.

Publisher: RODNEY FRIEDMAN • Editor: MARYA DALRYMPLE
Senior Editor: RACHEL D. CARLEY • Managing Editor: BRENDA SAVARD • Consulting Editor: CHARLES L. MEE, JR.
Writers: LAURA CERWINSKE, ROSEMARY G. RENNICKE • Freelance Writers: DARLYN BREWER,
DONNA CORNACHIO, MICHAEL McTWIGAN, JOE L. ROSSON, MARY SEARS
Design Editors: NANCY MERNIT, CATHRYN SCHWING
Test Kitchen Director: GRACE YOUNG • Newsletter Editor: BONNIE SLOTNICK
Editorial Assistants: SANTHA CASSELL, CAROLE McCURDY • Contributing Editors: ANNE MOFFAT,
DEE SHAPIRO, CINDA SILER • Indexer: IAN TUCKER

Art Director: JUDITH HENRY • Associate Art Director: SARA REYNOLDS
Designer: SARA BOWMAN • Assistant Designer: TIMOTHY JEFFS
Photographer: STEVEN MAYS • Photo Editors: ALICIA HATHAWAY, SUE ISRAEL
Photo Assistant: SIMEONE RICCI • Freelance Photographers: LAURIE BLACK, RON BRELLO, JR.,
JON ELLIOTT, DAVID GLOMB, STEVEN MARK NEEDHAM, BRADLEY OLMAN, DAVID PHELPS,
GEORGE ROSS, BILL WALDRON • Freelance Photo Stylist: VALORIE FISHER

Consultants: BOB CAHN, JACQUELINE DAMIAN, HELAINE W. FENDELMAN,
LINDA C. FRANKLIN, GLORIA GALE, KATHLEEN EAGEN JOHNSON, ELEANOR LEVIE,
JUNE SPRIGG, CLAIRE WHITCOMB

Time-Life Books Inc. is a wholly owned subsidiary of TIME INCORPORATED.

Founder: HENRY R. LUCE 1898-1967

Editor-in-Chief: JASON McMANUS • Chairman and Chief Executive Officer: J. RICHARD MUNRO
President and Chief Operating Officer: N. J. NICHOLAS JR. • Editorial Director: RAY CAVE
Executive Vice President, Books: KELSO F. SUTTON • Vice President, Books: GEORGE ARTANDI

TIME-LIFE BOOKS INC.

Editor: GEORGE CONSTABLE • Executive Editor: ELLEN PHILLIPS
Director of Design: LOUIS KLEIN • Director of Editorial Resources: PHYLLIS K. WISE
Editorial Board: RUSSELL B. ADAMS JR., DALE M. BROWN, ROBERTA CONLAN, THOMAS H. FLAHERTY,
LEE HASSIG, DONIA ANN STEELE, ROSALIND STUBENBERG, HENRY WOODHEAD
Director of Photography and Research: JOHN CONRAD WEISER
Assistant Director of Editorial Resources: ELISE RITTER GIBSON

President: CHRISTOPHER T. LINEN • Chief Operating Officer: JOHN M. FAHEY JR.
Senior Vice Presidents: ROBERT M. DeSENA, JAMES L. MERCER, PAUL R. STEWART
Vice Presidents: STEPHEN L. BAIR, RALPH J. CUOMO, NEAL GOFF, STEPHEN L. GOLDSTEIN,
JUANITA T. JAMES, HALLETT JOHNSON III, CAROL KAPLAN, SUSAN J. MARUYAMA,
ROBERT H. SMITH, JOSEPH J. WARD
Director of Production Services: ROBERT J. PASSANTINO

For information about any Time-Life book please call 1-800-621-7026, or write:
Reader Information, Time-Life Customer Service
P.O. Box C-32068, Richmond, Virginia 23261-2068

Time-Life Books Inc. offers a wide range of fine recordings, including a Rock 'n' Roll Era series.
For subscription information, call 1-800-621-7026, or write TIME-LIFE MUSIC,
P.O. Box C-32068, Richmond, Virginia 23261-2068.